THE REFERENCE SHELF (*Continued*)

Volume 28

No.

1. Immigration and the United States. Poyntz Tyler. $2.

2. Juvenile Delinquency. G. S. McClellan. $2.

4. Community Planning. H. L. Marx. Jr. $2.

No.

5. The Government and the Farmer. W. M. Daniels. $2.

6. The Middle East in the Cold War. G. S. McClellan. $2.

Volume 26

No.

5. The Censorship of Books. 2d printing. W. M. Daniels. $2.

Volume 24

No.

3. Representative American Speeches: 1951-1952. A. C. Baird. $1.75.

Volume 23

No.

2. Representative American Speeches: 1950-1951. A. C. Baird. $1.75.

Volume 22

No.

3. Representative American Speeches: 1949-1950. A. C. Baird. $1.75.

Volume 20

No.

5. Federal World Government. J. E. Johnsen. $1.50.

THE REFERENCE SHELF

Vol. 32   No. 5

THE SECURITY
OF THE
FREE WORLD

Edited by
JULIEN ENGEL

THE H. W. WILSON COMPANY
NEW YORK   1960

PREFACE

The start of a new decade always impels a glance back at the recent past, followed by a glance ahead. Such a stock-taking is the aim of the present collection of articles, which deals with the 1960-1961 high school debate and discussion theme designated by the National University Extension Association: *How can the security of the free world best be maintained?*

The view in either direction gave promise at the outset that 1960 would be a year of significant change. The outlook was moderately encouraging. The widely heralded Summit conference lay ahead. The Berlin crisis had at least temporarily abated. The Geneva disarmament parleys seemed likely to produce a limited accord between East and West.

There had, furthermore, been signs of new thinking and some significant developments with respect to two of the subjects proposed for debate and discussion: the United Nations and the North Atlantic Treaty Organization. These are dealt with in Sections II and III of this compilation.

Little could be said on the third discussion topic, World Government, that had not been said before. Indeed, it had virtually been withdrawn from the realm of public debate. But an allied concept, World Law, had recently been gaining attention. Accordingly, it became the burden of Section IV, not to the exclusion of World Government since that issue too, as will be seen, is quietly reemerging as a notable by-product of the disarmament-test ban negotiations.

By midyear, the modest optimism of the preceding winter had vanished: 1960's claim to historical fame was solidly established on a somber foundation of political catastrophes and propaganda setbacks such as the United States, and the entire free world, had seldom experienced before. A bare enumera-

tion will suffice: the U-2 affair, and the President's unprecedented assumption of responsibility for our openly-admitted
intelligence activities; the subsequent collapse of the Summit
conference in Paris; Premier Khrushchev's abrupt withdrawal
of the invitation for the President's state visit to the Soviet
Union; the liberal revolts against the increasingly despotic and
corrupt regimes of two political leaders closely identified with
American policy—President Syngman Rhee in South Korea, and
Premier Adnan Menderes in Turkey; the violent demonstrations
against Premier Nobusuke Kishi of Japan which nearly destroyed the new United States—Japan security treaty and forced
a last-minute cancellation of the President's visit to that country; finally, the Communists' surprise walk-out from the Geneva
disarmament negotiations rendering stillborn the new proposals
that the United States was about to submit in a move to break
the East-West deadlock.

This turn of events underscored the importance to free
world security of such questions as the aims of Soviet policy,
the feasibility of arms limitations, and the vulnerability of the
underdeveloped world. These are duly treated in Section I, V,
and VI below.

A word of caution. In speaking of the "free world," it
should be remembered that the term is commonly used to
describe the entire area not controlled in its basic policies by
Moscow or Peiping. Although these peoples may live under all
sorts of institutions, they are all free (including Communist
Yugoslavia) of Soviet or Chinese Communist domination. In
speaking of "security," it should not be forgotten that United
States military policy remains its prime determinant. The
absence of any discussion of that aspect of security in this book
is due simply to limitations of space.

The editor is much indebted to the staff of the Carnegie
Endowment for International Peace for an infinitude of cour-
tesies which very materially eased his task, and to his former
colleagues at the Foreign Policy Association—World Affairs

Center for many good turns and helpful suggestions. Thanks are also due to the various authors, publishers, and organizations for permission to use the materials included in this book.

JULIEN ENGEL

July 1960

A NOTE TO THE READER

For earlier surveys in the Reference Shelf series the reader should consult *United Nations or World Government* by Julia E. Johnsen (Volume 19, No. 5); *Federal World Government* by Julia E. Johnsen (Volume 20, No. 5); and *The United States and International Organizations* by Robert E. Summers (Volume 24, No. 5).

CONTENTS

PREFACE 3

I. EAST VERSUS WEST

Editor's Introduction 11
The Conditions of the Postwar World 12
Halle, Louis J. Soviet Aims Have Changed ....
.... New Republic 18
Soviet Aims Have Not Changed 22
Salisbury, Harrison E. U.S. and U.S.S.R.: The Dangers
Ahead .... Foreign Policy Bulletin 29

II. THE UNITED NATIONS

Editor's Introduction 37
Gross, Ernest A. The United Nations Record ....
.... New York Times Magazine 38
Beer, Max. Far-reaching Change of Membership ....
.... Swiss Review of World Affairs 44
Morgenthau, Hans J. The New United Nations ......
.... Commentary 47
An Independent Secretary-General .... The Economist 55
Wright, Quincy. How Can the UN Be Strengthened? ....
.... Foreign Policy Bulletin 58
Good, Robert C. A UN Police Force? ..... Commonweal 62
Jessup, Philip C. What the United States Should Do 67
Pearson, Lester B. The UN Between East and West ....
.... New York Times Magazine 71
Gross, Ernest A. No Alternative to UN ..... New Leader 74

III. NATO AT THE CROSSROADS

Editor's Introduction 76

Boone, W. F. NATO—Keystone of Defense ....
.... United States Naval Institute Proceedings   78
Webster, Sir Charles. The Record to Date ...... Listener   81
Howard, Michael. The Military Equation .... Listener   84
Buchan, Alastair. The Case for a NATO Deterrent ....
.... The Reporter   90
Buchan, Alastair. The Meaning of Interdependence   92
Middleton, Drew. The Question of Leadership: United
    States .... New York Times Magazine   99
Schumann, Maurice. The Question of Leadership: France
.... Réalités in America 104
Spaak, Paul-Henri. Political and Economic Policies ......
.... NATO Letter 109
Fischer, John. Military Policy—A Proposal ....
.... Harper's Magazine 114

IV. WORLD LAW AND WORLD GOVERNMENT

Editor's Introduction 124
Jennings, R. Y. What Is International (World) Law? ...
.... Listener 125
Nixon, Richard M. The Rule of Law for Nations ......
.... Vital Speeches of the Day 132
Mr. Nixon's Nostrum .... National Review 137
The Connally Reservation .... Life 139
Dean, Vera Micheles. Would World Law Avert War?....
.... Foreign Policy Bulletin 141
Up the World Government Path .... The Economist 142
Madariaga, Salvador de. World Commonwealth 146

V. CAN THE ARMS RACE BE CHECKED?

Editor's Introduction 149
Thomas, Hugh. Disarmament: Dream or Reality? ......
.... Political Quarterly 150
The Disarmament Plans Compared ...... New York Times 155

Harris, Seymour E. Economic Consequences of Disarmament
.... New York Times Magazine 157
Break-off of Negotiations .... New York Times 160
The Nth Country Problem and Arms Control 163
A Test-Ban Primer .... Time 165
Test-Ban Achievement at Geneva ...... New York Times 169
Rabinowitch, Eugene. Disarming Distrust ....
.... Bulletin of the Atomic Scientists 173

VI. UNDERDEVELOPED NATIONS: THE NORTH-SOUTH
      PROBLEM

Editor's Introduction 180
Hoffman, Paul G. The Underdeveloped World 182
Franks, Sir Oliver. A New Perspective for the Atlantic
      World .... Saturday Review 189
Soviet Expectations of the Underdeveloped Areas 193
Sulzberger, C. L. Russia's Cold War Battle Plan ....
.... New York Times 197

BIBLIOGRAPHY 200

I. EAST VERSUS WEST

EDITOR'S INTRODUCTION

If one were bold enough to offer a capsule characterization of the post-World War II era, it would have to be something like "universal ferment." For in no comparable span of human history has the old order changed so very swiftly, completely, irrevocably. A bird's-eye view of this sweeping transformation, and of our place at the threshold of the sixties, is presented in the selection which opens this chapter, from a study especially prepared for the Senate Foreign Relations Committee.

Some twenty years ago Sir Winston Churchill coined his famous phrase, "Russia is a riddle wrapped in a mystery inside an enigma." For all their accumulated knowledge and experience, and it is now quite considerable, experts on the Soviet Union—who have acquired such garish titles as Sovietologists or Kremlinologists—will find little to quarrel with in this definition.

Despite the vast liberalization in East-West relations since the death of Stalin, the proliferating exchange visits of politicians, specialists, and tourists, and the now relative ease of establishing contact with Russians of all stripes on their home grounds, the most baffling question of our age remains, "What is Soviet Russia up to?" and conjointly, "How should we deal with it?"

As may be seen from the second and third selections—one presenting the view of a perceptive political analyst and former member of the State Department policy planning staff, the other the distilled thinking of some of the leading American scholars of Soviet affairs—there is room for honest difference of opinion on the answer.

A typical example of this groping-in-the-dark for an understanding of Soviet behavior is furnished by Harrison E. Salisbury's analysis of the hidden forces which drove Premier Khrushchev to torpedo the long-awaited Summit conference in May. While each expert may have his own pet explanation, and there probably are as many of these legitimately held as there are experts, most will agree that the downing of a high-flying American U-2 aircraft on a photo-intelligence mission deep into Russia provided the excuse rather than the cause for the spectacular Paris turn-about in Soviet policy.

THE CONDITIONS OF THE POSTWAR WORLD [1]

The choice for responsible and continuing participation in world affairs was one of the great decisions in the history of our country. From it came the establishment of the United Nations, America's leading role in the world's recovery from the destruction left by the war, and the sense of purposeful commitment to the principles of freedom and justice for which the American people had fought.

It soon became apparent, however, that the new world order was not going to be orderly at all; that forces of tyranny and aggression were active in a new quarter of the globe; that many new and revolutionary forces were making themselves felt; that both the American people and those specifically charged with the formulation and conduct of U.S. foreign policy would have to develop a greater understanding of the nature of those forces; and that new "great decisions" would have to be made. The major developments of the past fifteen years, though familiar to many, need to be recalled to mind in order to illuminate the aims, and the needs, for the future.

Soviet Power and Expansionism

The combination of great power and expansionist ambitions represented by the Soviet Union—to which were added by 1949 the European satellites and Communist China—has posed the threat that this massive agglomeration of power would continue to expand into other areas and threaten the security of the United States itself. Violating its agreements, the Soviet Union

[1] From *United States Foreign Policy: Basic Aims of United States Foreign Policy, a Study,* prepared at the request of the Senate Committee on Foreign Relations by the Council on Foreign Relations. United States. Senate. Committee on Foreign Relations. 86th Congress, 1st session. Supt. of Docs. Washington 25, D.C. '59. p 2-6.

refused to restore their independence to the Eastern European states its armies had overrun in the course of the war. It converted temporary lines of occupation into rigid territorial barriers separating the Communist from the non-Communist world. It maintained vast military power and subjected other states to threats and pressures aimed at territorial changes or political submission. It refused to agree to a peace settlement which would end the division of Germany, and without a settlement on Germany no stable settlement for Europe as a whole could be achieved. Confident of the ultimate victory of communism throughout the world, the Soviet leaders have followed a persistent and dynamic policy of expansion. They have used a variety of means, including, in the case of Korea, direct military aggression by satellite forces. While Soviet tactics vary from time to time, mixing blandishments and talk of peace with threats, the world has no reason to count on basic changes or on internal developments that will weaken the economic, political, or military power of the Soviet regime or change the main direction of Soviet policies.

China Under Aggressive Communism

China, which the United States hoped to see a strong and friendly ally, has come under Communist domination, except for Taiwan and a few small islands remaining under the control of the Chinese Nationalist Government. Mainland China has risen rapidly since 1949 from a position of near helplessness to one of great strength under the direction of a Communist regime allied with the Soviet Union and from the start deeply hostile to the United States. Its policies toward many countries on its borders, some of them closely associated with the United States, have been overbearing and aggressive, and in one case (Korea) it deliberately embarked on open warfare against United Nations forces under American leadership.

Impotence of the United Nations

The conflict which came to be known as the cold war has proved beyond the capacity of the United Nations to prevent or control. Because of the basis on which the organization was established, action to check aggression or threats to the peace rests on the unanimity of the great powers, a condition which has seldom been attainable since 1945. Thus there has been no international authority through which the principle of collective security could be made consistently effective against direct or indirect aggression on the part of the Soviet Union or Communist China. The United Nations did play a significant role, however, in certain of the postwar crises, in support of that principle: in Korea, where it assumed responsibility for the military operations taken under American leadership to resist aggression; in the Suez crisis, where resolutions of the General Assembly led to the cessation of military action by Britain, France, and Israel, and the UN Emergency Force helped in the liquidation of the affair; and in a number of cases involving nations other than major powers where the authority of the United Nations was exerted to bring an end to hostilities. The Uniting for Peace resolution and the work initiated by the Collective Measures Committee at least opened the possibility that the United Nations might be able to take effective action in spite of a veto in the Security Council. But in facing the realities of the postwar period the United States and other nations have had to look primarily to regional groupings and to policies of self-defense in order to find ways of protecting the free world.

Conflicts Within a Reborn Europe

Western Europe, an area vital to the security of the United States and linked to it by common values for which both had just fought, was in a state of great weakness in the early postwar years. By themselves the Western European nations could not regain their economic health, nor could they maintain their security except through new forms of association among themselves and with the United States. As a result of far-reaching measures of recovery and cooperation begun under the Marshall plan and with the establishment of NATO, Western Europe has registered a remarkable growth in productivity, strength, and cohesion. Despite this considerable progress, the over-all strength and unity of Western Europe continue to be hampered by conflicts of national policies and of economic interests, evident for example in the unsettled economic relationship between the six nations of the European Economic Community and the other nations outside it.

Nationalism in Africa and Asia

A revolution has taken place in the former colonial and less developed areas of Asia and Africa. Many new nations have won their independence, with others sure to follow; the drive for independence in Africa is much stronger and more rapid than was expected. These nations have acquired a special importance in world affairs for a number of reasons: strategic location, large and growing populations, resources (such as oil), their insistence on rapid economic development, and above all the magnitude of their own problems, to which the rest of the world cannot be indifferent. Political stability has been hard to achieve, as the exercise of self-government proved a more complex task than the attainment of it. The working out of new relationships with the industrial countries has been a particularly difficult process on both sides. Attitudes stemming from the past relationship of dependence did not easily disappear, especially at a time when Communist powers were making strong and not unsuccessful efforts to extend their influence into these areas. Endeavors of the United States to establish a basis of cooperation with the Asian and African nations have been complicated by its association with the former colonial powers, by local conflicts such as the strife over Palestine, and by wide differences of view on the nature of the Communist threat and what to do about it.

Instability in Latin America

Latin America, although outside the main theaters of the cold war, has been beset by political and economic instability and by the problems of adapting its institutions to rapid social change. It is apparent that the attitudes and policies of the United States may be crucial in determining whether the growth and travail of the Latin American countries will be a controlled revolution taking place without disruption of the inter-American system and the Atlantic community, or whether they will become the scene of uncontrollable unrest and cold-war competition.

The Balance of Terror

The gradual shift from possession of an atomic monopoly toward a position of virtual nuclear parity with the Soviet Union deprived the United States of a significant military advantage. It could no longer regard its massive striking power as so effective a deterrent to aggression or as a guarantee of victory at acceptable cost in the event of the ultimate test of war. The growth of Soviet nuclear power, together with the maintenance of huge conventional forces in the Communist bloc, has compelled the United States and other free nations to be prepared for a wide variety of military moves the Communist powers might make, from the fomenting of civil conflict to the launching of all-out war. Because of the need for a global military posture adequate for deterrence and for the necessary operations if deterrence failed, the United States has had to sustain a peacetime military effort of unprecedented size and cost and has also sought new relationships with a large number of countries based on common efforts for mutual security.

The Question of Arms Limitations and Controls

The pace of technological change led to weapons of such destructive power that both the United States and the Soviet Union have had to consider whether the arbitrament of total war could be accepted even as the ultimate means of preserving vital interests and national security. Nuclear weapons and their delivery systems, however, have taken their place beside other weapons within the existing scheme of world politics, which is in essence a conflict between two great blocs over the control or denial of territory, involving on both sides an intricate complex of strategic plans and calculations, fears, warnings, commitments, and considerations of prestige. Thus, while the possession of the means of massive destruction by both sides has produced a situation of mutual deterrence, total war remains a real possibility, whether resulting from a direct military challenge to the territory of one bloc or the other, miscalculation, or a local conflict which could get out of control. The Soviet refusal to accept an adequate system of inspection and control has made it impossible to reach agreement on an international system of arms limitation which would reduce or eliminate these terrible prospects. But the United States can take little comfort in assigning blame for the deadlock to the Soviet Union. The urgency of finding some means to control nuclear weapons and other armaments remains.

The Changing Environment

In addition to its application to weapons, the march of science and technology is rapidly changing the environment in which all nations live, without necessarily respecting or conforming to the political and other relationships which have grown up over the centuries. The accelerating pace of change has upset traditions, created new demands, encouraged revolutionary ferment. It affects what nations want and what they can or cannot do. Increasingly, their problems have gone far beyond handling as matters of purely national policy. The interdependence and interpenetration of societies requires reassessment of what is meant by such terms as sovereignty and nonintervention. Governments find themselves dealing primarily with complex situations, with wide-ranging political and economic forces, not just with relations with other governments. Man's ventures into space call into question existing legal and political concepts. Such problems as are involved in the production and use of the world's resources of energy and raw materials have forced many nations, including the United States, to face new choices on how to work out relations with each other and with existing or new regional groupings, how to modify or expand international economic institutions, and whether to seek the basis of a new world order. Scientific advance, with its promise of plenty, brings not only new problems but great new opportunities.

SOVIET AIMS HAVE CHANGED [2]

In the years after Stalin's death all of us debated the question whether any real change had taken place in the nature of the Soviet challenge. The widespread anxiety among us to deny it was exceedingly human. Like a football team trying to keep up the old spirit, we urged one another not to be taken in by smiles or soft words from Moscow. We repeatedly announced that there was no evidence of any change. We repeated, until it became ritualistic, the statement that Moscow, however it might have changed its tactics, had not renounced its objective of world revolution. Since the foreign policy which we had established after long and strenuous efforts had been entirely a response to the Soviet challenge as manifested under Stalin, the alternative to such an insistence on the changeless nature of the challenge might have been to see the bases of that policy crumble. This was, and it continues to be, our real and understandable fear.

I do not suppose that the Soviet society underwent any abrupt and fundamental change on the date of Stalin's death. But fundamental changes have been taking place continuously, as in every society, so that the question for us to ask is rather *what* than *whether.* . . .

The actual events of history [have] failed to confirm the predictions . . . [of Marxian ideology]. I shall mention here two fundamental expectations of the Communist fathers that the actual experience of history has now disappointed, and I shall suggest the revolutionary (or counterrevolutionary) consequences.

The first expectation to be disappointed was that the proletarian masses everywhere would come to side with international communism against their capitalist rulers and accept the leadership of the Communist elite. Under that leadership they would at last rise up of their own will to overthrow capitalism and, with it, all the sordid apparatus of national states, imperialism and militarism. . . . Instead, in the great industrial countries capital and labor have tended to resolve the class struggle and have

[2] From "Has the Soviet Challenge Changed?" by Louis J. Halle, former U.S. State Department official. *New Republic.* 140:9-11. Je. 22, '59. Reprinted by permission.

increasingly reached an accommodation that has satisfied the welfare and self-respect of labor. The sharpness of the class distinctions has tended to disappear, and this has made capital and labor allies in their opposition to the would-be leadership of the Communist elite. Instead of becoming more revolutionary, the working masses have in fact become antirevolutionary. . . . The Communist movement has not been able to win the allegiance of the world's proletarian masses. . . .

Stalin met the failure of the prediction to come true by imposing his personal dictatorship inside Russia. . . . Communist rule . . . [was] spread beyond the Soviet Union only by the Red Army, in support of whatever successes of sabotage and subversion . . . [were] achieved by Communist agents in each country. If the masses would not respond to the Communist leadership of their own accord, then they would have to be conquered. . . .

The other expectation of the Communists, which history has disappointed, existed primarily as a tacit assumption. Since, in Marxian doctrine, all the workers of the world are brothers, national divisions being merely the contrivances of their class enemies, all the societies resulting from the Communist revolution must share a harmony of purpose and policy. Any society captured by the international Communist movement would naturally be an ally of the Soviet Union (even after the Soviet Union had resumed, under Stalin, the trappings and regalia of a national state). It would be in Moscow's camp, loyal and valiant in the struggle to overcome Moscow's enemies. Apparently nobody before 1948, on either side of the Iron Curtain, gave much thought to the possibility of such a thing as the development of national communism outside of Russia. Then Tito's Yugoslavia demonstrated the fact that Moscow could not count on the implicit obedience or cooperation of any independent state, beyond the effective reach of the Red Army, simply because it was Communist. It demonstrated the fact that such a state might put its own nationalism first.

The implications of this demonstration, in terms of the Communist world that was originally projected, seem to me immense. It put in question all the hopes that Moscow had once attached to the prospective enlargement and eventual universalization of the Communist world. Appreciating all the implications of this lesson, Moscow today might well prefer a neutralized and non-Communist Austria to a Communist and potentially "Titoist" Austria; it might prefer a Finland to a Hungary as its neighbor; it might in time come to wish that the Communist revolution had not occurred in China; and it is not inconceivable that the thought of a Communist United States would occasion nightmares in the Kremlin. If the world were Communist, there is no reason to believe that its capital would be Moscow—even if it did have only one capital.

Neither World Revolution Nor Conquest

When the nature of the Communist challenge is discussed today we still tend to repeat that Moscow has not given up its objective of world revolution—just as if a proclamation to that effect was what we were waiting for. But I should suppose that Moscow has in fact given it up as a working objective, however much its spokesmen . . . still, occasionally, give lip-service to it. I should suppose that the question for us to ask now is whether Moscow has, as an alternative, set itself the objective of world conquest.

I suggest that the answer to this question too, in terms of the working objectives of the men in the Kremlin, is no. Opinion varies on the weight of the burden that the indefinite control of the restive satellite populations puts on Moscow. Perhaps the burden is still far from capacity. Perhaps Denmark and Sweden could be added to it; perhaps Norway and Holland; perhaps Italy and France; perhaps the British Isles. But somewhere there must be a limit and, in any case, the prospect of such an empire, seething with rebellion, must seem quite different from the prospect of a spreading revolution by the masses themselves which Lenin and his associates looked forward to in 1917. It must give the military and political chiefs in the Kremlin pause. And today, if they were offered the choice of a satellite France or a France on the model of Finland, perhaps they would choose the latter. A commanding position in the world might seem more attractive than the direct ownership of the world.

Has the nature of the Communist challenge, then, changed? I suggest that it has, and that one of the changes is the abandonment of either world revolution or world conquest as a practical objective.

The bulk of the evidence indicates that, when Stalin's successors took over, they looked at the empire he had bequeathed them and found it already overextended. Like the Emperor Hadrian coming into his inheritance in 117 A.D., they decided that the time was ripe, not only to stop the expansion, but for retrenchment and consolidation. They thereupon gave up Austria, which Stalin had been trying to capture; they gave up Yugoslavia; and they took steps in the direction of restoring the independence of Poland and Hungary. They went too far too fast, and when what was intended as a limited retreat threatened to turn into a total rout they had to abandon it.

If these suppositions are correct, then the objectives of Moscow today represent a continuation of those Russian national and imperial objectives that may be traced back at least as far as the beginnings of Muscovy in the twelfth century. They represent this rather than the anti-nationalistic, anti-imperialistic and revolutionary objectives which Lenin, Trotsky and Company had set themselves. They are the old objectives of achieving security for Russia by pushing back the hostile military powers that have always surrounded her. In the long historic course of pushing those powers back, the territory under Russian control has at last expanded to its present inordinate dimensions. And still the drive continues, now taking the form of opposition to NATO bases in Turkey, Greece, Italy, Scandinavia, West Germany and other parts of Europe.

Such an objective, though far from being the same as that of world conquest, implies unlimited expansion, since Moscow can never reach the point of full satisfaction. It must always be impelled to extend still further the area from which it can exclude threats to its security. Therefore, Russia's neighbors must, in the future as in the past, be strong to resist. But the problem that is posed for them, as for Moscow, is a familiar one. It is the old problem of establishing a stable equilibrium of forces and a modus vivendi which provides at least the minimum of security that each side must have in order to accept it. This requires a sober and peaceable, but a firm diplomacy, backed by adequate force and determination.

There is reason to believe that it is such an equilibrium as this that Premier Khrushchev and his associates are aiming at today. Such an equilibrium as this is also a proper immediate objective of our own Western policy. But, even though both sides alike wish to achieve it, it will not be easy to achieve, as the present difficulties over the status of West Berlin show.

And we must recognize that when it is achieved, . . . we must still be prepared for that continuation of competition in the sphere of economic and political rivalry which our opponents refer to when they talk of "coexistence," competition which confronts us with a challenge that, within reasonable bounds, we would do well to accept as legitimate. And, when it is achieved, its maintenance will still depend on our ability to keep up our strength.

SOVIET AIMS HAVE NOT CHANGED [3]

In recent years, the nature of the problem presented by the Soviet Union has been changing in certain important respects. The Soviet leadership, confident in the massive growth of the Soviet economy and technology, looks forward to a decisive increase in Soviet power and influence in the world. The Soviet problem needs to be understood not only in its military dimensions and as a problem of political and economic penetration in various parts of the world, but also as a challenge to the way in which our society organizes the use of its human and material resources.

[3] From *United States Foreign Policy: U.S.S.R. and Eastern Europe, a Study,* prepared at the request of the Senate Committee on Foreign Relations by a Columbia-Harvard Research Group. United States. Senate. Committee on Foreign Relations. 86th Congress, 2d session. Supt. of Docs. Washington 25, D.C. '60. p 1, 5-6, 16-17, 21, 53-4.

Although the emphasis in current Soviet policy is upon "peaceful coexistence," Mr. Khrushchev has reminded us quite frankly that this line does not mean a suspension of the underlying conflict between our societies. This conflict grows out of the Soviet commitment to the transformation, sooner or later, by one means or another, of non-Communist states to "socialism" and then "communism," as the Soviet Union uses these words.

[The question is] whether this source of conflict is moderated by recent changes within the Soviet Union. . . . The evidence seems to suggest that these internal changes are not likely, at least over the next decade or so, to lead to real normalization of Soviet relations with the rest of the world. Despite the possibility of crises, domestically and within the orbit, the position of the Soviet leadership promises to remain strong and its commitment to Communist goals unimpaired.

As a consequence, if present trends continue, a further increase of Soviet power and influence is to be expected.

Dealing with the Soviet challenge should not become an exclusive preoccupation of American policy. While it is of vital importance that we steadily take the measure of the Soviet challenge, without becoming distracted by the day-to-day ups and downs of Soviet "atmospheric" changes, the central focus of our policy should be the political growth and economic improvement of the non-Communist world. This forward movement, inspired by a vision of democratic progress, is essential to the creation of a world environment favorable to the survival and development of free institutions. It is also the course of action most likely to lead to a modification of Soviet policies over the long run. . . .

What the Soviet Union Expects of the 1960's

Perhaps the best place to begin, in thinking about our relations with the Soviet Union, is with a clear understanding of what the Soviet leaders expect to happen in the world in the years immediately ahead, and what they intend Soviet policy to accomplish. This is not as obvious as it seems. Mr. Khrushchev and other Soviet leaders have tried to explain to us what they think is happening. In the spirit of a chess player who tells what he is going to do because he is certain his opponent is helpless to avert a checkmate, Mr. Khrushchev told us over and over again during his visit to the United States what he had meant by saying, "We will bury you." So far, however, the people of the United States have not absorbed this information into their thinking and are far from having reflected an awareness of it in their national policy or their foreign policy. Mr. Khrushchev thinks that this is no accident, that our society is incapable of responding to the conditions now existing in the world. This merely reinforces his confidence that Soviet expectations will be realized.

The single most essential fact about the outlook of the Soviet leaders is that they see the world in a process of transition, in which one social order has outlived its usefulness and is being replaced by a new one. This process they believe to be an inevitable one, determined by the "laws of history" but requiring their active aid. They identify the declining social order as "capitalism" or, in its advanced stages, "imperialism." The rising new form of social and economic organization they call "socialism," or, in its ultimate development, "communism." With characteristic vigor, Mr. Khrushchev has said: "Capitalism is a worn-out mare while socialism is new, young and full of teeming energy." In the Soviet view, the world is divided into two camps, one representing declining capitalism and the other rising socialism; and between these two camps a fundamental and inevitable conflict exists. This conflict need not result in war, but whether it does or not depends primarily upon whether capitalism is graceful or stubborn about recognizing that it is outworn. Peacefully or not, the result is bound to be the world-wide triumph of "socialism," that is, of the Soviet system. The next stage of history, already begun in the Soviet Union, will then be the transformation of "socialism" into "communism."

This is, in its simplest form, the nub of the problem. Of course, for our part, we do not agree with the way Mr. Khrushchev sets up the problem, nor with his use of words. In our view, what the Soviet system represents is not "socialism" as we understand the term, nor a representation of "working-class interests," but a totalitarian state governed by a dictatorial party. From our point of view, the essential quality of our system is not "capitalism," but freedom. But what matters here is to understand what the Soviet leaders mean when they use these words, and how they perceive the fundamental nature of the conflict.

A question which is often argued is whether the Soviet leadership is motivated more by ideology or by practical considerations of national power. Without resolving this question in its generalized form, it is possible to make the practical observation that since the world-wide triumph of "socialism" would mean that the Soviet Union would become the dominant world power, there is no conflict between Soviet national power considerations and the Marxist-Leninist view of the process of social transformation of the world—so long as "socialism" is defined, as it is in Soviet ideology, as the rule of Communist parties acting on common principles and with the discipline of a single camp directed by the Soviet Union. What this approach to the problem emphasizes, however, is that the simplified image sometimes advanced in the West of the Soviet leadership as a group of conspirators out to rule the world by military conquest or by plotting violent revolution does not sufficiently explain the full nature of the challenge. In the Soviet outlook, the workings of underlying social processes are the fundamental condition to which their policy is directed. Military conquest, subversion, and violent revolution have all been used by the Soviet regime, and may be used again, but they are only some of the possible ways by which the further transformation of the world is to be realized. The adequacy of our response depends, above all, upon our understanding first, that this is not simply a challenge of possible military attack or of political subversion but also a deadly contest between different ways of organizing society and using resources, and, second, that the Soviet commitment to the transformation of non-Communist states into Soviet-style states, by whatever means and by whatever name, is a dynamic commitment which, so long as it is maintained, is not subject to stabilization, especially in these times of rapid and far-reaching social change. . . .

So long as Soviet objectives remain unlimited—that is, if they can be realized only by the elimination of our non-Communist forms of government—then a resolution of the conflict is possible only if we are willing to yield to the Soviet Union what it wants. Whatever changes in the climate may take place, or whatever settlements of specific issues may become possible, should not be allowed to obscure the reality of this underlying condition of deadly conflict. . . .

It is possible to make the following practical judgment as a guide to our actions. Much as we, as individuals, may dislike the Soviet system, the proper point of concern of our national policy is not with the internal organization of the Soviet Union but with Soviet behavior in the world. It is the Soviet commitment to the inevitable transformation of all other states to the Soviet system, by whatever means, that is the essential cause of ineradicable conflict. If this commitment were to change with time, the fundamental conflict would be eased, or at least it would no longer have its present unlimited character. . . .

Whether time will have an effect upon Soviet totalitarianism is conjectural, . . . but in any case it is the question of the unlimited expansionism of Soviet policy which is the point to which we must direct our concern.

But can this struggle be waged on some plane other than war? This is what Mr. Khrushchev is asking. It seems reasonable to believe that the Soviet leaders do now have a serious realization of the destructiveness of nuclear weapons, that they would genuinely prefer to achieve their objectives without total war, and are confident that they can do so. It is less certain what the response of the Soviet leaders would be if their choice were between total war and a decisive loss of important objectives. Our past experience with Soviet policy does not encourage the belief that the Soviet Union has given up for all time the use of force or the threat of force as an instrument of policy.

This much seems clear: If we are to insure that the threat or use of force will not become a decisive element in this conflict, it is essential that a serious imbalance of military capability must not be allowed to develop.

One of the central purposes of American foreign policy since the "cold war" began has been to get this confrontation onto some ground less dangerous to the human race. What we have not done, however, is to appreciate what is required of us in the realm of political and economic competition if we do succeed in keeping the military factor from being the decisive one.

Whether we call it "peaceful coexistence" or "cold war" . . . does not matter as much as understanding that what is involved is a continuum of conflict in varied forms. Perhaps the Soviet slogan of "peaceful coexistence" is a useful one if it succeeds in directing our attention to the distinctive requirements of the present phase of Soviet policy. The phrase "cold war" has taken on the coloration of the period of the militant Soviet challenge of the immediate postwar years. It seems to suggest to people's minds a response which is purely military, sterile, and static, instead of the sense of the forward movement of a vital society in all its manifestations, which is the only true answer to the present phase of the Soviet challenge. . . .

The conception of "peace" used by the Soviet leadership . . . is based upon the nonresistance of the rest of the world to the changes anticipated, desired, and assisted by Soviet policy. One can grant that Mr. Khrushchev may be perfectly sincere— undoubtedly is—in his desire for peace in this sense. But the effect of such Soviet actions as the satellization of Eastern Europe, the Berlin blockade, and the present threat to Berlin is to increase the danger of war unless the non-Communist world remains unresponsive or acquiescent toward these expansionist actions.

Moreover, the history of Soviet policy . . . shows an alternation between periods of militant pressures and conciliatory gestures, as alternative ways of advancing Soviet interests under changing conditions. It would require a very short memory for the rest of the world to act upon the assumption that Soviet policy cannot again return to a phase of military pressure.

Although the Soviet leaders may be genuinely concerned about the risks of war, the possibilities of the destruction of cities in the Soviet Union, the setback to their hard-won achievements;

and although they may prefer to achieve their objectives in the world by peaceful means, and are now confident they will do so—the question remains what they would do if it appeared to them that their confidence was mistaken, that the tide of history was flowing (even though temporarily, in their view) adversely for the Soviet position in the world. Mr. Khrushchev has left no doubt that he would fight rather than relinquish a foot of territory now under Communist control. If this adverse trend were to come at a time when the Soviet leaders were convinced of their own military superiority, could the rest of the world afford to put its faith in the restraint of the Soviet leadership? . . .

We do not seek to preserve the status quo in the world. We agree with Mr. Khrushchev that the world is in the midst of revolutionary changes, but we think he is wrong in believing that these changes point only in the direction of Soviet communism. We are conscious of the fact that nationalism and technological change are profoundly altering the present relationships among states, but we do not have a commitment to some foreordained pattern of a new world order. We are in the midst of a process of trying to find new forms of collaboration between states, new patterns of trade, of economic development, of political cooperation. We believe deeply in pluralism, at home and in the world. We believe our interests are sufficiently served if there is opportunity for growth in a variety of ways toward political freedom and economic progress.

The cause of our conflict with the Soviet Union is that we must resist the Soviet effort to achieve a uniform Soviet solution for the world and Soviet control over other nations. To meet and overcome this challenge does not express our central purpose, any more than the purposes of a man's life are fulfilled by overcoming a disease. The foreign policy objectives of the United States are not definable in the framework of the Soviet problem, but in terms of what it seeks to do despite the Soviet challenge.

The American purpose in regard to the Soviet Union is a limited, and essentially protective purpose. We welcome any changes in the Soviet Union that may ease for the Soviet people the burdens of totalitarianism, and we hope these will continue in the future, but it is not within our power to intervene in Soviet internal affairs to achieve our purposes. We recognize the technological and economic achievements of the Soviet regime, and, on a separate plane from our moral judgment about police-state methods, we recognize that it represents an alternative form of organization of society. This is not, however, the cause of conflict. The issue is not, despite Mr. Khrushchev, "socialism" or "communism" versus "capitalism." The issue is to be found in the universalist and unlimited objectives of Soviet policy, which must be resisted until they are changed.

With his usual clarity, the French journalist and scholar, Raymond Aron, has put the point in this way:

> Should the Soviets ever recognize that their regime is only one of a number of possible ways of organizing industrial societies, the majority of democrats—while continuing to regard certain practices of the Soviet regime as deplorable, inefficient or inhuman—would no longer feel obliged to maintain an attitude of active hostility to the Soviet Union.

U.S. AND U.S.S.R.: THE DANGERS AHEAD [4]

The prime danger of the failure of the Paris conference is the impetus it seems certain to give to tendencies within both the U.S.S.R. and the United States, leading back toward the worst tensions of the cold war.

While it is true that the cold war has never ended, there had been in the past two or three years a measurable relaxation of East-West tensions. Mutual suspicions had by no means been wiped out. But they had been reduced to more manageable proportions.

Now, the Paris events have given powerful momentum to a new direction in international relations—back toward the Stalin era. Neither side may actually desire to return to those grim days. Both sides may be well aware of the catastrophe which is inherent in another "deep freeze" when both sides have nuclear arms and intercontinental rockets. . . .

[4] From article by Harrison E. Salisbury, New York *Times* expert on Russia, in *Foreign Policy Bulletin*, published by Foreign Policy Association-World Affairs Center. 39:145-7, 150. Je. 15, '60. Reprinted by permission.

It seems imperative that we examine with the greatest care
the actual factors which produced the Paris disaster. At best
we are headed for difficult times; at worst for mutual annihilation. Whatever policy we adopt we should understand as precisely as possible its probable effect upon Moscow. Will it
strengthen the hand of Premier Khrushchev? Will it play into
the hands of the Chinese Communists? Will it assist in bringing into power leaders who will be less difficult or more difficult
to deal with?

It now seems clear that two sets of factors were involved in
the failure of the Summit. We are painfully familiar with the
first set—the U-2 flight and the way it was handled in Washington.

But there was another set of circumstances—the delicate
balance of forces at the pinnacle of Soviet power—which played
perhaps an even more important role and which we have peril-
ously disregarded.

The first thing to recognize is that Premier Khrushchev was
far from being a free agent as he approached the Summit. Because he is a dictator and a successful leader of the Communist
party we tend to conceive of him as all-powerful and able to
do as he pleases.

No dictator is a completely free agent—not even a Stalin
or a Hitler. Mr. Khrushchev is a ruthless politician who since
Stalin's death has usually managed to get his way. But this has
not been easy for him, and there has never been a time when
he did not have opposition within his own leadership group as
well as from other powerful spokesmen within the Communist
world.

Power Struggle in U.S.S.R.

It can now be documented with very little difficulty that in
the weeks before the Summit Mr. Khrushchev and his policies
were the center of a major struggle behind the scenes in the
Kremlin.

Men usually seek explanations of events from their own experience. In describing American policy on Berlin Mr. Khrushchev said:

"Apparently an underground and complicated struggle of different political forces was going on in the United States of America. It caused grave apprehensions."

Mr. Khrushchev's words described most precisely what has been happening in the Soviet Union. This Communist argument has not been carried on in a vacuum. It has been affected by outside forces. One of the factors which strongly affected the outcome was American policy. And, it seems certain, American policy operated against our own best interests by weakening Mr. Khrushchev's case for negotiating with the West. Inadvertently we strengthened the hands of his Stalinist opponents who had opposed him from the start.

There are those who contend that Mr. Khrushchev's actions at Paris were a logical outgrowth of past policy; that he had never intended to negotiate with the West; that his interest in genuine relaxation of tensions was insincere.

This not only overlooks the elaborate, stubborn, and energetic campaign which Khrushchev conducted for more than three years to get into negotiations with the West. It casts aside the forceful and even violent arguments which the Chinese Communists have been publishing, particularly in recent months, against the idea that negotiation with the West was even possible.

There have been various explanations for Khrushchev's drive for a *détente* [lessening of tension] with the West. Some have suggested that he needs relaxation in order to attain his domestic goals. Others have seen him taking the first steps toward providing Russia with a Western exit in the event that Communist China grows too big and too belligerent.

Moscow's "Decompression"

His whole philosophy of decompression at home and abroad was staunchly opposed by Foreign Minister Vyacheslav M. Molotov on grounds of fundamental Marxist doctrine. Molotov opposed the Austrian State Treaty. He opposed the *rapprochement* with Marshal Tito. He opposed what he regarded as Khrushchev's adventurous policy in the general field of foreign affairs.

Mr. Khrushchev's quarrels with Molotov were not the only ones he had. The disputes with such men as former Premier Georgi M. Malenkov and Lazar M. Kaganovich over increased incentives for collective farmers, the virgin lands program, decentralization of industry were not mere personality clashes. They involved basic Communist principle.

Mr. Khrushchev in 1957 triumphed over a coalition of all his Communist party Presidium enemies and sent them into banishment. But he never really eliminated what for want of a better word may be called his Stalinist opposition. He retained Mikhail A. Suslov, the old Stalinist propagandist, within the inner circle. Probably Mr. Suslov was too valuable to spare because of his influence with Stalinist personnel and the Chinese Communist party leadership.

For three years Mr. Khrushchev, aided and abetted by Anastas I. Mikoyan, assiduously promoted the idea of *détente*. But his Marxist critics would not be stilled. When in the summer of 1958 Mr. Khrushchev was on the point of going to New York for a "summit" meeting of the United Nations Security Council (which he had proposed) he suddenly called the whole thing off after taking a hurried trip to consult his Chinese allies in Peiping. The conclusion was inescapable that Peiping vetoed the trip.

Finally the long and arduous path toward the Summit seemed to have been opened up.

But the closer the Summit approached the more apparent it was that there were active opponents of the policy within Mr. Khrushchev's camp. Mr. Suslov became more active, and even more active was a group of propagandists associated with him. The propagandist group traveled with Mr. Khrushchev wherever he went—to the United States, to France, to Indonesia and to the abortive Summit. These men made no secret of their skepticism about the West. It was they who created a witch hunt for "anti-Soviet" books at the American exhibition in Moscow, who coached the hecklers whom Vice President Nixon encountered on his trip to Russia, who sought out slights, incidents and "provocations" to Mr. Khrushchev during his United States trip.

More ominous were the reactions of Peiping. The better relations got between Moscow and the West the sharper grew Peiping's policy toward India, Tibet, Burma and Indonesia. If Mr. Khrushchev wanted a *détente* and lessened world tensions it was more and more obvious that China wanted just the opposite.

Mr. K's Opponents

In this situation Mr. Khrushchev's position was not as strong as it appeared on the surface. . . . [He] continued to propagandize vigorously for negotiations with the United States. He issued books, brochures, films and posters designed to popularize the idea that he had laid the foundations for successful negotiation in his trip to the United States and his talks with President Eisenhower.

But his propaganda had little or no effect upon the Communist Chinese. Peiping continued to spew forth violent anti-American denunciations reminiscent of the worst days of the cold war.

As early as the time of Mr. Mikoyan's trip to the United States in January 1959 some American advisers had recommended that Washington make more positive gestures of cordiality toward the Khrushchev overtures. Their argument was that Mr. Khrushchev's policies had vigorous opposition in Moscow. Unless the United States reciprocated, they argued, Khrushchev might easily lose out in the Presidium debates.

Little was done at that time. When Mr. Khrushchev finally arrived in America President Eisenhower gave him real encouragement, but, thereafter, Washington lapsed into inaction until March, when both Secretary Christian A. Herter and Undersecretary Dillon made what Moscow interpreted as "hard line" speeches.

By this time a comparison of the Moscow and Peiping propaganda lines would have clearly disclosed danger signs. Peiping was getting tougher. Moscow was raising questions. In mid-April Mr. Khrushchev sent a trusted aide, Georgi A. Zhukov (not the marshal), chairman of the state committee on cultural relations, to New York and Washington to take soundings on whether the United States had "changed its policy" and did not propose to negotiate in good faith at the Summit.

Debate within the Kremlin over Mr. Khrushchev's policy unquestionably was rising. Mr. Zhukov's mission reflected this. . . .

It may be that the Soviet armed forces joined in the discussion at this point. . . . It is certain that a good deal of military antagonism toward Mr. Khrushchev was engendered by his January proposals for the forced retirement of 200,000 to 300,000 members of the officer corps. Suslov was in charge of the propaganda drive to sell this program to the officers. He may have made common cause with them.

Ten days before the fatal U-2 flight on May 1 the Chinese Communist press blossomed forth with a whole series of articles about basic Marxist policy. These constituted thinly veiled criticisms of Mr. Khrushchev's whole theory of leadership. They cast into gravest doubt the theory of negotiation with the West, the idea of a Summit conference and the sincerity of President Eisenhower personally.

Even at this point, it seems apparent, Mr. Khrushchev still retained command of the situation and still hoped to go to Paris and negotiate, although perhaps with sharply reduced expectations.

Effect of U-2

But he stood on slippery ground. There had been a coalition of influences against him, and it was in these circumstances that the U-2 incident occurred with such devastating consequences.

It seems doubtful that Mr. Khrushchev had any real choice at this point. He either had to go over to the policy of his critics or be pushed out.   Agile politician that he is he undoubtedly decided to jump before he was shoved.

This decision sealed the fate of the Summit.   But there are substantial reasons for suspecting that worse may lie ahead. Mr. Khrushchev has for all practical purposes been forced publicly to repudiate the policy of negotiation to which he had so firmly committed himself in the face of stubborn and powerful Marxist arguments by his opponents.

After the U-2 incident Mao Tse-tung observed in Peiping, "No unrealistic illusions should be cherished with regard to imperialism.   Some people had described Eisenhower as a man who cherished peace.   We hope that these people will be awakened by these facts."

Chairman Mao's remark, of course, was directed squarely at Mr. Khrushchev, who sponsored the concept of Eisenhower as the man of peace—against all prejudices of the classic Marxists.

The internal pressures to hold Mr. Khrushchev to an increasingly harder and tougher Marxist-Stalinist-Maoist line will be powerful.   He is a stubborn and skilled politician.   Often in the past he has been able to return to a basic policy even though temporarily diverted.   But it will be far harder this time. Indeed, he may have taken the first steps toward political downfall.

Questions for the United States

Is this the result which the authors of American policy had in mind?   Do we really think a Suslov would be better to deal with than a Khrushchev?   Do we really want Russia moving onto the hard, intransigent tracks of Maoist communism?   Can we really look forward with equanimity to a strengthened alliance of Soviet industry and ultra-modern technique with China's one-billion-by-1975-population potential?   Is it the objective of our foreign policy to produce another Stalin?   Are we prepared to face the foreign and domestic consequences of a new and far more dangerous cold war?

To ask these questions is to answer them. Naturally, we want none of these. Yet, by our own policy we have given the Communist world a powerful thrust in the direction of all the things we do not want. Mr. Khrushchev, as we well know, is a most difficult man. But he is hardly likely to be as difficult as his successor.

In the selection of a national foreign policy we do not have any more of a free choice than Mr. Khrushchev does. But there is a choice between lesser and greater evils.

Considering the dangers involved, it seems obvious that we must attempt to fashion our tactics in such a way as to create, if possible, conditions which are more, rather than less, favorable to ourselves and our survival. Often we are not precisely aware of the relative balance of forces within the Communist world. But survival dictates that we sharply reduce our margin of past error.

II. THE UNITED NATIONS

EDITOR'S INTRODUCTION

Those who are weary or cynical may claim that the United Nations grew straight from awkward youth into jabbering senility without an intervening stage of mature achievement.

Without conceding to so despairing a view, this section does present a clinical diagnosis of the several ailments and complications that have marred the UN's health since birth, keeping frail and ineffectual what should have become humanity's stout defender of the public order. Particularly astringent in its analysis is the selection by Hans J. Morgenthau, a political scientist well known for his hardheaded probing into world organizations. He finds little that is encouraging in the condition of our patient. Yet, one recent development—explored in the succeeding article, from *The Economist*—appears to hold some promise. This is the increasing political influence and initiative exercised by Secretary-General Dag Hammarskjöld, in a manner neither foreseen nor provided for in the Charter but made necessary by the paralysis of the Security Council and the timidity of the General Assembly.

In the remainder of this section, among the prescriptions for restoring the UN to its intended role, Quincy Wright advances four "approaches" that require no tampering with the Charter. His final proposal, for a UN police force, is followed by a critical examination of this perennial favorite, with the perhaps surprising finding that such a force would be a mixed blessing at best.

Philip C. Jessup catalogues certain practical steps that the United States could immediately take, in concert with other nations, to strengthen the international organization, while Lester B. Pearson and Ernest A. Gross, both with long experience at the UN, conclude with generally optimistic assessments of its potential. The former stresses the many intangible ways in which the UN does make its presence felt, and draws attention to its virtually unlimited future in the social, economic, and humanitarian fields. The latter warns that there is no real alternative to the UN and that inspired leadership can do much to redress its oft-deplored weakness.

THE UNITED NATIONS RECORD [1]

In 1945 at San Francisco, after a generation of unprecedented collective insecurity, the world turned to the United Nations as a cure for the diseases of international society. Today, almost half a generation later, the need for a rudimentary world order grows ever more apparent. Yet it is asked: Is the UN adequate to its purpose? Is it doomed to futility?

These questions have deep roots. They arise partly because of misconceptions of the nature and purposes of the UN and partly from the failure of the member nations to use fully and effectively the instrument their own governments established.

The misconceptions were born of the hopes and sufferings of the world as expressed by the statesmen who gathered at San Francisco. Even so great a realist as Sir Winston Churchill had earlier voiced his conviction that "the most intense effort will be made by the leading powers to prolong their honorable association." Much disillusionment stems from the frustration of this hope.

Within the limits of its structure, the UN can point to solid achievements. It has helped to avert war and halt aggression. And it has helped young nations find their place in the world.

Yet the cold war and the armaments race center in the UN forum, and there is a long catalogue of disputes which remain from year to year on the UN's agenda of unfinished business.

This sketchy balance sheet, in itself, illustrates the gap between people's hopes and a realistic appraisal of what the UN is. The organization does not have the attributes of a state, to say nothing of a super-state. The architects of the UN did

[1] From "U.N. Record and U.N. Dilemma" by Ernest A. Gross, former United States ambassador to the United Nations. New York *Times Magazine.* p 12, 69-71. S. 21, '58.

not seek to build an ark against the flood. They devised procedures whereby a somewhat ragged convoy of sovereign states might assemble, sail together on stormy seas and, when need be, find safe anchorage.

Talk of "successes or failures of the United Nations" is superficial at best. As Secretary-General Hammarskjöld has declared:

When the UN is said to have scored a success, this obviously means only that intended results have been reached in making use of the forms of negotiation the organization offers. And when it is said that the UN has failed, this means conversely that it turned out that what was desired could not be reached through these forms of negotiation.

The question remains: How can the UN be more effectively used for its intended purposes? The answer must be found in an appraisal of the record and the prospects.

To begin with, there is no doubt that the UN has been used with some success in what might be called the *strategy for peace.* It has served to reconcile parties to political conflict which had threatened, and indeed in some cases, actually precipitated war. Kashmir and Indonesia are leading examples. The UN has been used also to channel nationalist unrest which might have flooded into revolution. Half a dozen new states have been assisted into the world with relatively painless births. Israel survives under the shelter of a UN supervised armistice. Korea, reduced for a moment by aggression to a beachhead at Pusan, regained its homeland under the UN flag.

In the second place, the UN and its specialized agencies have, to a degree at least, been useful in building the *economic foundations of peace.* The UN "Expanded Program of Technical Assistance" covers ninety countries and territories although it disposes of only thirty million dollars annually. At the last session of the General Assembly, the decision was reached to set up a United Nations Special Fund, for development assistance. There has also been cooperation through the UN in the development of peaceful uses of atomic energy. Members of the organization, including all the atomic powers, convened the 1955 scientific conference on atomic uses. This produced an important breakthrough in the exchange of information and research. A second conference . . . proved to be of even larger scope than the first.

Then, there have been steps, though not without some recent faltering, toward use of the UN in building the *foundations of human freedom.* We do not hear much about the UN Declaration of Human Rights, yet its provisions are incorporated in the constitutions of several new states. The work of UNESCO is becoming better understood and respected, except on the part of a few who do not care to know the facts.

Another service the UN provides is that of a forum for debate. Derision of the United Nations as a "debating society" is as wide of the mark as the obsolete quip that a Parliament is merely a *"gouvernement qui parle"* [a government that prattles]. Public debates in the UN can serve a vital function.

They have served the free world by unveiling the objectives of the Kremlin leaders. In 1952, the Communists demanded the forcible repatriation of Korean prisoners of war. Andrei Y. Vishinsky, then Soviet Foreign Minister, declared before the bar of public opinion that the individual had no will higher than the will of the state. The despotic nature of the Communist system stood revealed as if by lightning.

On the positive side, an effective use of the forum was the day in December, 1953, when President Eisenhower made his "Atoms for Peace" address in the General Assembly. . . He evoked an electric response. Moreover, he achieved the practical effect of all good debate. The Soviet Government was induced, by the pressure of informed public opinion, to negotiate seriously. As a result, the International Agency for Atomic Energy is in being—one of the few fruits of East-West cooperation.

Finally, the UN has afforded the means for continuing negotiation to an extent practicable only in a multilateral forum. Any UN delegate will confirm that 95 per cent of his working time is spent far from microphone and camera, much of it in "consultation," which is merely a word to describe negotiation among friends.

Soviet intransigence has indeed produced frustration, as in the . . . disarmament negotiations. But even in this area, the value of a standing diplomatic conference with a permanent secretariat has been shown. Through quiet initiative, the Secretary-General succeeded in bringing about negotiations in Geneva between U.S. and Soviet scientists to develop methods for policing a ban on nuclear tests. . . . The same procedures [might be followed] in connection with our "open skies" proposal. . . .

United Nations history is strewn with the wreckage of lost opportunities lying in the wake of the cold war. There are, in the main, three principal dilemmas.

It is fruitless to speculate on why the Soviet leaders adhered to the Charter in the first place. That their action in doing so was rooted in cynical self-interest is clear from the fact that they have been in contempt of its principles from the beginning. The first dilemma arises from the fact that the convoy of nations must include the Communist states, including Red China ultimately, for it would be even more dangerous to leave them free to prowl like pirates with atomic cannon.

Another dilemma which tests our leadership, and consequently the effectiveness of the UN, arises from unfulfilled nationalist aspirations and social unrest. We are caught in a crossfire of friends, torn between sympathy for those young nations who demand freedom and respect for those older ones who have furnished the very vocabulary of freedom.

The most cruel dilemmas of all are those combining the first two: when the Communist revolt against the Charter takes the form of feeding—and feeding upon—the forces of national and social ferment. These are situations which, as Stalin once boasted, "contain unexhausted revolutionary possibilities," and provide openings for subversion or, as it is now commonly called, indirect aggression.

The principles of the Charter require that any lawful state or regime, however unstable, be free from externally directed violence or subversion. Yet the line between what is fomented from abroad and what is fermented from within is hard to draw, as the history of our own Revolution, as well as most others, makes quite clear. This presents hard decisions to states like ourselves, which seek to use the UN as an instrument for orderly changes in the status quo.

When we felt impelled by the unexpected coup in Iraq [in 1958] to land United States marines across the Beirut beachhead as the British dropped paratroopers into Jordan, something more profound took place than a mere "holding action." The shift from collective action to unilateral intervention brought on an entire new set of navigational problems. Unilateral action—however well intentioned—by its nature rallies extremists, puts moderates on the defensive and is unsettling and divisive. . . .

In contrast, the invited presence of representatives of an international body or of its Secretary-General tends to strengthen the elements of stability in troubled areas and thus helps build self-discipline and unity. Moreover, the UN presence helps deter indirect aggression by focusing public attention upon the foreign sources of subversion and the means used to incite violence.

In the late 1940's, experience showed the value of UN observation and supervision in helping find time for forces of stability to take hold. The Balkan Commission in 1947 helped preserve the independence of Greece by spotlighting her frontiers. The UN Korean Commission at once reported aggression, thus facilitating the urgent Security Council move on the fateful Sunday in 1950.

Later that same year, the fourteen-member UN Peace Observation Commission (POC) was organized as a permanent body to "observe and report," upon the request of the General Assembly or the Security Council, in any area of dangerous international tension. John Foster Dulles . . . hailed the POC as "the eyes and ears of the United Nations." Yet as Secretary of State he . . . [did] not once . . . [suggest] that it be called into service, and in fact it has been dormant since 1951.

During the few days when Imre Nagy held power in Hungary and besought help, a UN observation group might well have been rushed to the spot from near-by capitals. Its presence would have had great moral value and it might perhaps have been able to offer asylum to the entrapped leaders of the revolt. Even the UN "eyes and ears" failed Hungary in her hours of tragedy. . . . A new outlook which views observation and supervision as a *routine UN function* is just as important as the fabrication of a new mechanism in the diplomatic machine shop. . . .

One way of bringing the Secretary-General's power more in line with his duties would be to authorize him, on his own motion, without the need for prior approval by the General Assembly or Security Council, to appoint commissions to observe and supervise in areas of tension. In keeping with democratic processes, his nominations might be made subject to confirmation by a standing committee of the General Assembly, perhaps in the form of a renovated Peace Observation Commission. Moreover, such a commission might be encouraged to set up agencies to go to troubled areas, without awaiting Assembly or Security Council action.

An additional method of strengthening the hand of the Secretary-General, at the same time increasing the use of another major organ of the UN system, the International Court of Justice, would be to empower the Secretary-General at his own discretion to request advisory opinions in disputes or situations involving justiciable issues. The Soviets would no doubt veto such an amendment to the Charter but there is nothing to preclude other states from making such an agreement among themselves.

As for the UN's future role in building the economic foundations of peace, the UN economics budget now is little more than a good-will offering. About $12 million annually is allotted in the UN budget for: all regional economic activities, administration of all economic and human rights programs, narcotic drugs control, world-wide statistical work and the administration of displaced persons programs (other than Palestinian refugees). Although the UN technical assistance activities and the work of its specialized agencies are effective, the financial contribution of the United States to such multilateral programs is only about $65 million, less than 1 per cent of our annual defense budget. At the very least our existing mutual security program should make increased use of the United Nations. We could rest assured that recipients would none the less know where most of the money came from.

Finally, larger sharing through the UN of our science and technology would help us, as well as the organization, play a more positive role.

FAR-REACHING CHANGE OF MEMBERSHIP [2]

Today, eighty-two nations belong to the world organization—thirty-one more than at the time of its foundation. No longer do the twenty Latin-American countries together with European and Commonwealth countries assure the United States of a two-thirds majority in the Assembly. The strongest group now is that constituted by the twenty-nine African and Asian countries which—apart from those allied with the West, like Japan, Turkey, the Philippines, Iran and Thailand—act as a compact bloc on many issues. This group can frequently count on the votes of the ten Communist countries—the Soviet Union, its eight satellites and Yugoslavia—as well as on a growing number of Latin-Americans that will no longer be fitted into a bloc with North America. Small Europeans like Iceland, Eire, Finland, Sweden and occasionally Austria also are close to this group, which thus is becoming increasingly capable of either preventing the formation of majorities or making or preventing diplomatic combinations and compromises. It is not simply its numerical weight, but also its political and propagandistic weight, its uninhibited dynamism and elementary methods which provide it with a strength such as no other group in the Assembly commands. In the next few years it will be enlarged by about ten new members—Cameroon, Togoland, Somalia and Nigeria [as well as the Congo and the eleven states of the French Community—Ed.] will in fact already become members in 1960. Apart from the new Republic of Cyprus, no new addition is to be expected from Europe, on

[2] From "The Changing United Nations" by Max Beer, UN correspondent. *Swiss Review of World Affairs*. 10:20-22. F. '60. Reprinted by permission.

the other hand, while the Latin-American as well as the white Commonwealth memberships have already reached their maximum limits. Antagonisms which no "relaxation" can reduce or eliminate among and within some of these groups—even within the group of the NATO nations—continuously increase the Afro-Asian group's opportunities.

The transformation of the General Assembly and the UN is particularly revolutionary in that the front is now occupied not by countries with long experience and developed civilizations, like Japan, India or Lebanon, but by the young and youngest nations of Black Africa which are still in a state of ferment and eager to federate. Sure of an early increase of their numerical strength, and sure of the opportunities offered them in shifting their support back and forth at will between East and West, they display a degree of self-confidence which at times threatens to shake the very structure of the world organization. Undoubtedly not all the tirades of the African leaders need to be taken seriously. Also, Afro-Asian solidarity is not without fissures, either, and many an Asian or Mideastern country is irritated by its black brothers' brashness. Even the Soviets may begin to consider the forces, which at present they exploit to their own advantage, with somewhat different eyes later on. Nevertheless, the awakening of Africa is methodically promoted by the United Nations and has become an established fact of far-reaching consequences. . . .

This development was even less foreseen by the founders of the United Nations than the cold war and the atomic and hydrogen bomb. It has completely changed the relations between continents, races, economies and civilizations in the United Nations. Delegates who speak in the name of highly developed countries are outvoted, and forced to compromise with delegates who, while themselves perhaps civilized, represent large amorphous and often illiterate masses. In 1960 the UN is no longer what it was in 1945 and throughout the first decade of its existence. If ever there was a "second League of Nations" at all, the third is now in the making.

At Stake: The Future of the United Nations

What, under these circumstances, will its future fate be? Will an attempt be made to reestablish the old equilibrium by restoring the Security Council to its role as the organization's principal agency? The enlargement of the Council that will become inevitable in a few years is bound to reflect the described transformation also. And for how much longer will the interventions of a shrewd and discreet Secretary-General correct the inability of this or that part of the UN to take useful decisions?

Some people hope that gradually a balance will develop between the forces of the old world and the new nations of Asia and especially Africa, in political, economic, and cultural respects. In this connection they also consider the possibility of some understanding being arrived at between East and West, since without this the former will hardly be possible. . . . They expect much of the calm, the wisdom, and the will to sacrifice of the free world which, however, in order to be able to fulfill these expectations, ought to be freed of the nightmare of the danger of war.

On the other hand, the number of those who call for more insight on the part of the leaders of the dynamic new nations as well as of the Communist countries is also growing. At the time of the decline of the old League of Nations it was often stated that its continuation and its success depended on the will and the ability of each individual member to *make use of it*. Perhaps this statement might be rephrased with reference to the United Nations, to say that it can continue to exist and remain successful only if every member is *finding it useful*. Neither the Africans nor the Communists would in the long run stand to benefit if more and more nations of the free world were to become convinced that the organization is of no use to them, but on the contrary weighing them down with insoluble problems which they would not, or at least not in so acute a form, come up against without it. Undoubtedly it is a good thing that Guinea is in the United Nations and can raise its voice there without hindrance. But it is not a good thing that a situation arises in which France loses interest in collaboration. It is probably inevitable that the demands made on the organization will continue to grow all the time, and that Communist China will finally have to be made a member. But it would be sheer folly to forget that without a proportionate influence by the largest, wealthiest, and most progressive democracy of the world, there can be no real United Nations.

THE NEW UNITED NATIONS [3]

In trying to assess the contribution the United Nations makes today, and might be able to make tomorrow, to the settlement of international conflicts, it is indispensable to keep in mind that what we call the United Nations today is not what the United Nations started out to be. A sharp distinction must be drawn between the constitutional provisions of the Charter and the manner in which the agencies of the United Nations, under the pressure of unforeseen political circumstances, have actually performed their functions under the Charter. What we habitually do with regard to the government of the United States we must also do here: confront the provisions of the constitution with the realities of political practice. Nor does our task end here. For within this sphere of political practice we must also clearly distinguish between two phases in the development of the United Nations: one covering roughly the first decade of the organization's existence, the second starting in 1957. The United Nations of the first phase differs in its character and the functions it was able to perform from the United Nations of the second phase, as both differ from the United Nations envisaged by the text of the Charter.

The Charter intends the United Nations to be an international government by the great powers, which are identified as the five permanent members of the Security Council, i.e., China, France, Great Britain, the Soviet Union, and the United States.

[3] From "The New United Nations: What It Can't and Can Do" by Hans J. Morgenthau, director of the University of Chicago's Center for the Study of American Foreign Policy. Reprinted from *Commentary*. 26:375-82. N. '58. Copyright American Jewish Committee.

Two major constitutional devices serve that purpose. Articles 10 to 14 establish the predominance of the Security Council over the General Assembly by limiting the latter to the making of recommendations in political matters. The General Assembly can debate, investigate, and recommend, but it cannot act. Even these functions are qualified by Article 12, which precludes the General Assembly from making even recommendations on matters that are on the agenda of the Security Council. This device enables the Security Council to control indirectly the political functions of the General Assembly. By simply putting a matter on its agenda, the Security Council can transform the General Assembly into a debating society without even the right to express its collective opinion on the matter.

The predominance of the Security Council having thus been established, the Charter proceeds to establish the predominance of the great powers within the Security Council. Article 27, paragraph 3, stipulates that "decisions of the Security Council . . . shall be made by an affirmative vote of seven members including the concurring votes of the permanent members." That is the famous veto provision. Dissent by one of the permanent members is sufficient to prevent action by the Security Council, even when all the other ten members are in favor of it. In other words, each of the permanent members has a veto. Thus the Charter predicates the United Nations upon the continuing unity of the permanent members of the Security Council. In the scheme of the Charter these five members are, as it were, the nucleus of a world federation, of a limited world government. It follows that with but one permanent member dissenting there can be no international government of the United Nations.

Actually, however, the international government of the United Nations is government by the great powers to a still greater degree than the foregoing analysis would indicate. Of the five permanent members of the Security Council only two, the United States and the Soviet Union, are really great powers. Great Britain and France are medium powers, China is only potentially a great power, and the government of Formosa, which occupies the permanent seat of China, represents the mere fragment of a nation. Under the present conditions of world politics, most members of the Security Council, the permanent members included, can be prevailed upon, if need be, to support a position taken by both the United States and the Soviet Union. The international government of the United Nations, stripped of its legal trimmings, then, is really the international government of the United States and the Soviet Union acting in unison. At best— if they are united—they can govern the rest of the world for the purpose of maintaining order and preventing war. At worst—if they are disunited—there will be no international government at all.

This constitutional scheme was built upon three political assumptions. First, the great powers, acting in unison, would deal with any threat to peace and security, regardless of its source. Second, their combined wisdom and strength would be sufficient to meet all such threats without resort to war. Third, no such threat would emanate from one of the great powers themselves. These assumptions have not stood the test of experience. The great powers have not been able to act in unison when their divergent interests were at stake, which is another way of saying that they have been able to act in unison only in rare and exceptional circumstances. And the main threat to the peace and security of the world emanates from the great powers themselves.

Thus the constitutional scheme of the Charter, defied by the political reality of the postwar world, has remained a dead letter. The conflict between the United States and the Soviet Union has prevented the United Nations from becoming the international government of the great powers which the Charter intended it to be. That conflict has paralyzed the Security Council—placing the United States and the Soviet Union generally on opposite sides of the issues voted on—and is responsible for the ascendancy of the General Assembly as the dominant political agency of the United Nations. These two complementary developments are graphically demonstrated by the quantitative decline of the activities of the Security Council and the corresponding increase of those of the General Assembly. The Security Council started out, in accordance with the intention of the Charter, by meeting more often and dealing with more political issues than the General Assembly. After reaching the pinnacle of its importance in 1947-1948, its activities declined steadily until the London *Economist* could say at the beginning of 1958, mixing its metaphors a bit: "The almost lifeless skeleton of the Council stands like a blasted rock in the background of the UN scene."

The General Assembly owes its present dominant position primarily to the inability of the Security Council to perform the task with which the Charter charges it: preserve peace and security. The impotence of the Security Council and the need for the General Assembly to take its place became dramatically obvious during the Korean war. With the Security Council paralyzed by the Russian veto, the General Assembly passed in November 1950 the "Uniting for Peace" resolution which established the General Assembly as the main United Nations agency for the preservation of peace and security.

In view of the text of the Charter, the General Assembly should never have been able to supersede the Security Council in any respect. For the Charter erects a seemingly insurmountable obstacle to any such usurpation by giving only the Security Council the power to make legally binding decisions and by allowing the General Assembly to do no more than recommend. The ever more marked inability of the Security Council to decide has brought about a subtle change in the relative powers of the two agencies. This change has endowed the recommendations of the General Assembly with an authority akin to that of a legally binding decision. The overwhelming majority of the members of the United Nations have felt that the United Nations ought to take action with regard to certain matters and that, in the absence of a Securiy Council able to act, the General Assembly ought to act in the manner the Security Council would have acted were it able to do so. Thus, while technically speaking the General Assembly can only recommend, a substantial majority of the members have shown a tendency to act upon these recommendations as though they were legally binding decisions.

This transformation of the General Assembly into the politically dominant agency of the United Nations was possible only because at least two-thirds of the member nations favored it. If at least a two-thirds majority had not voted for the recommendations which were submitted to the General Assembly during the last decade, that transformation would not have taken place. This majority is the instrument which has brought this transformation into being, which gives the transformation life as long as it supports it, and which determines its content and its strength. And it is upon the composition of that majority that the character of the transformation depends.

The composition of the majority supporting the recommendations of the General Assembly has undergone a drastic change with the admission of twenty new members in 1955-1956. This date constitutes a turning point in the history of the United Nations, closing one phase and ushering in a new one. It can even be said that the United Nations which existed before that date was a different instrument of international government from the United Nations existing today, capable of performing different functions from those which the present United Nations is able to perform. The transformation the United Nations has undergone has not stopped with the shifting of the center of political decision from the Security Council to the General Assembly. It has created within the General Assembly itself two different types of international organization, built upon two different kinds of majorities.

The majority which carried the recommendations of the General Assembly until the end of 1956 had as its nucleus the United States, the nations of Western Europe, most members of the British Commonwealth, and the Latin American nations, amounting to thirty-nine votes. Around this nucleus other nations grouped themselves in ever changing configurations, sometimes voting with the majority, sometimes against it, sometimes abstaining. Permanently excluded from it was the Soviet bloc, numbering five votes. Not only was this new United Nations an international government conducted without the participation of the Soviet bloc, it was also an international government which opposed the Soviet bloc as the latter opposed it. It owed its very existence, and found its main political and military purpose, in the opposition it offered to the Soviet bloc. In its purpose it could well be called a grand alliance directed against the Soviet bloc.

The increase in the membership of the United Nations from the original fifty to the present eighty-one [with Guinea, now eighty-two—Ed.] members has drastically changed the distribution of voting power in the General Assembly and, with it, the political functions the United Nations is able to perform through the General Assembly. The increase in membership has led to three politically significant changes in the distribution of votes. The Western bloc, counting forty-three votes, has lost its ability to marshal regularly a two-thirds majority in support of resolutions directed against the Soviet bloc. While it is still able to gain this support sporadically, as for instance in the resolutions dealing with conditions in Hungary, the nations which can be counted upon to support its policies with regularity number more than one-third but less than two-thirds of the total membership. In consequence, the best the United States can hope for with any degree of regularity is to impose a veto upon objectionable resolutions by withholding the vote of its supporters from them. The United States can still perform a negative task: prevent the use of the United Nations against its interest. But it can no longer count upon using the United Nations for the positive task of promoting its interests.

While the influence of the United States within the United Nations has thus drastically declined, that of the Soviet bloc, amounting to nine votes, has increased. During the first postwar decade, the Soviet Union was in a virtually hopeless minority, both in the Security Council and the General Assembly. In the Security Council it has been able, as we have seen, to protect itself against the consequences of being regularly outvoted through the use of the veto. In the General Assembly it was unable as a rule to prevent resolutions objectionable to it from passing because it could count upon less than one-third of the members to support its position. Today, the Soviet Union has a good chance—although not yet as good a chance as has the United States—to add to the votes of the members of its bloc the votes of a number of other nations, which votes together would amount to more than one-third of the membership and would thus place the Soviet Union in a position to prevent resolutions objectionable to it from being passed.

This shift in the distribution of voting strength results from the fact that the massive increase in the membership of the United Nations primarily benefited nations belonging to the so-called Afro-Asian bloc. The Afro-Asian bloc, numbering . . . [thirty] members, comprises more than one-third of the membership of the United Nations. Thus, if it were to vote in unison, it could both exercise a veto on any resolution adverse to its interests or else, by joining either the American or the Soviet bloc, become the core of a working two-thirds majority. In reality, however, the Afro-Asian bloc has but rarely voted as a unit; its vote has typically been split, with some members voting with the Americans, others with the Soviet bloc, and a very considerable number abstaining. Consequently, as concerns the ability of the United Nations to function politically through the General Assembly, the Afro-Asian bloc has thus far performed a negative function. By splintering its vote between them, it has strengthened the power of the American and Soviet blocs to oppose the will of a simple majority with the veto of more than one-third of the membership. As a result, the General Assembly has proven itself incapable of passing resolutions calling for any action more decisive than investigations, good offices, and reports by the Secretary-General, his representatives or a committee of the General Assembly.

The sole exception is the resolution of February 3, 1957, establishing a United Nations emergency force to patrol the borders of the Gaza strip and the coast line adjacent to the straits of Tiran. Yet this action was due to a unique convergence of circumstances: the United States voting with the Soviet Union against its principal allies on a political issue, the general indifference if not hostility in the United Nations to the interests of Israel, the need of Egypt to recover from the rout of the Sinai campaign. Each of these positions commanded wide voting support, and their convergence assured overwhelming support for the action taken. In addition, the issue with which the General Assembly had to deal—mitigation of the danger of war at the two most sensitive spots of the Israeli Egyptian frontier—was susceptible to the limited action taken.

None of the issues that have come before the General Assembly since show either the convergence of positions supporting for different reasons the same action, or that susceptibility to a limited action, the only kind which the United Nations is capable of taking. Consequently, the General Assembly has had to limit itself to passing declaratory resolutions which at best convey the appearance of action while being devoid of substance. That appearance has been supplied by the office of the Secretary-General.

The Charter intends the Secretary-General to be "the chief administrative officer of the organization." He "may bring to the attention of the Security Council any matter which in his opinion may threaten the maintenance of international peace and security." And he "shall perform such other functions as are entrusted to him by (the) organs" of the United Nations. It is from this provision of the Charter that the new functions of the Secretary-General as the apparent chief political agent of the United Nations derive.

These new functions are intimately related to the impotence of the General Assembly, as the responsibility for action which the General Assembly has taken on is intimately related to the impotence of the Security Council. And one can go one step further and say that the responsibility for the settlement of political issues with which the United Nations as a whole has been burdened is a by-product of the inability of the nations directly concerned, especially the great powers, to settle outstanding political issues among themselves. The nations directly concerned and, more particularly, the great powers, have been unable to agree on a political settlement for the Middle East. So they charge the United Nations with finding a settlement. The members of the General Assembly, taking the place of the paralyzed Security Council, are no more able to agree on a settlement collectively than they were when acting as individual

nations.   So they charge the Secretary-General with finding a
solution.   Yet the result is bound to be not action delegated, but
inaction concealed.

AN INDEPENDENT SECRETARY-GENERAL [4]

The members of the United Nations might be unwise to
count on perpetual happiness if they go much further along the
road signposted "Leave it to Dag." The Secretary-General's
magic wand has lately been bestowing blessings so readily that
the beneficiaries are in danger of taking their continuance for
granted.

Since Mr Hammarskjöld succeeded Mr Trygve Lie in 1953,
remarkable changes have occurred in the way his office is regarded—by the Secretary-General himself as well as by others.
. . . Mr Hammarskjöld . . . was accepted as a neutral personality from a neutral country: a technician rather than a politician,
competent rather than dynamic, a man from whom more discretion than valor could be expected.   His preference for words of
diffuse caution seemed especially reassuring to those who had no
wish to see the UN secretariat become an independent force in
world politics.

How completely things have changed may be seen from his
. . . [1959] intervention in Laos [which claimed that Communist guerrilla bands were overrunning its frontiers and threatening its life]. Before he went there in November, Russia gave official and public warning that his visit was unwanted and suspect,
and specifically objected to any idea of his leaving behind a UN
representative there. He went, just the same; and while in Laos
he called in Mr Tuomioja, the Finnish secretary of the UN
Economic Commission for Europe. Mr Tuomioja is still in Laos,
and other UN officials are digging in there to look after the
long-term economic aid programs and administrative improve-
ments that he has recommended.

Mr Hammarskjöld . . . acted in Laos without any mandate
from the Assembly or the Security Council. . . .

[4] From "Mr. Hammarskjöld, We Presume." *The Economist*.   194:12-13.
Ja. 2, '60.   Reprinted by permission of *The Economist*, London.

This is the most ambitious expression yet of the philosophy which Mr Hammarskjöld has quietly but firmly developed since his renewal in office two years ago. When, on September 26, 1957, he accepted a further term, he made his first placidly revolutionary statement. He frankly declared that it would be fully in accordance with the spirit of the UN Charter for him to act without a mandate from either Assembly or Council, if he judged it necessary "to help fill any vacuum that may appear in the systems which the Charter and traditional diplomacy provide for the safeguarding of peace and security." His claim went unchallenged. So, in July, 1958, he could cite it in support of his independent decision to enlarge the observer corps in Lebanon after the American landing there. Russia had already vetoed both an American proposal to enlarge the corps and a Japanese proposal that he should be given a free hand to do whatever was needed to make an American withdrawal possible. The Swedish government, moreover, publicly demanded that the UN corps be removed. Mr Hammarskjöld calmly enlarged it; and there were no further objections.

Meanwhile he had also enlarged what one might call the Hammarskjöld Doctrine. On April 29, 1958, he told the Security Council that he welcomed the American proposal for an Arctic inspection system to discourage surprise attacks. He protected his flank by recalling that he had previously welcomed the Soviet announcement of a suspension of nuclear tests; but that did not save him from a sharply critical Russian reaction. One may guess that Moscow was particularly annoyed because he now claimed a right to voice the desire of the peoples of the whole world, and thereby trespassed on Mr Khrushchev's pet monopoly. And since then, the Secretary-General has progressively elaborated his claim to speak for common humanity, if need be in opposition to the views of all the major powers put together.

Just before the Geneva conference of four foreign ministers last year, he told a Copenhagen audience on May 2 that he had the right to take up an independent position based on "United Nations opinion" about any particular conflict, and to "express

what may be called the independent judgment of the organization." By October 16 he was speaking, in a television interview,
of the UN's role vis à vis the powers in regard to disarmament
as "an element representing all the rest of the world."

He has become increasingly open about his new role. In the
same interview, when asked on what he based his power to intervene in troublesome areas, he explained that the limitations of
the Assembly and Council made it necessary "to create a new
executive responsibility somewhere. . . ."

My own view is that they have defined the outer limit, and everything
which is, so to say, comprised within that limit is in line with the
philosophy of the Charter. In fact it is on the basis of this interpretation that quite a few recent developments have taken place, also on my
own initiative.

His initiatives have been of undoubted value. Whether despatching a personal emissary to look into the . . . Siamese-Cambodian
dispute, or smoothing the way for more British-Saudi discussion
of Buraimi, or quietly nagging Cairo about the holding up of
Israeli cargo in the Suez Canal, he has been using his unique
office to do things that can hardly be done by anybody else. In
so doing, he has built up a formidable body of precedent. Governments are beginning to realize this; but it is difficult to catch
him out.

Mr. Hammarskjöld can already claim a triple basis of his
policy. Not only is he expressing the *vox populorum,* and filling
"vacuums" where both the Charter and conventional diplomacy
are inadequate; he is now also able to point out that he is doing
things of a kind that he has done, with general approval, or at
least with tacit consent, before. Broadening down from precedent to precedent, his freedom of maneuver has far surpassed
the expectations of the governments that elected him. One may
be sincerely grateful for the good use he has made of this enlarged role, and yet concerned about the implications.

His successor may show less judgment of what is wise and
practicable (and Mr Hammarskjöld is not immortal, nor is he
necessarily in office for life). His judgment may fail him; the
world already has to reckon with too many situations where too
much depends on the health and good sense of one man. More-

over, if the UN members come to rely too heavily on his skill and his capacity for survival, they will neither give him adequate support nor overhaul their own practices so as to lessen his load. . . . There is much that could be done to support his ventures and relieve their loneliness; and little sign . . . that anybody is bothering to think about it.

HOW CAN THE UN BE STRENGTHENED? [5]

The United Nations could be strengthened by four approaches which do not involve amendment of the United Nations Charter.

(1) Reduction of the Influence of Crusading Ideologies in International Relations

The major obstacle to effective action by the United Nations in the political field has been the division of the world between the ideologies of Marxist communism and democratic liberalism.

This division has encouraged the development of rival "collective self-defense" blocs—NATO and Warsaw—each suspected of aggressive intentions by the other. The results have been extreme instability of the power equilibrium, mutual fears of attack, an arms race, increasing international tension, inability of the veto-ridden Security Council to function, establishment of blocs in the General Assembly distorting its reflection of world public opinion, an absence of the spirit of tolerance called for by the Charter, incapacity of representatives of the principal states to examine international problems on their merits, and involvement of most international conflicts in the "cold war," which makes their peaceful solution exceptionally difficult.

This situation has been partly ameliorated by some reduction in Soviet tyranny and expansionism since the death of Stalin, by the common conviction manifested at the Geneva Summit conference in 1955 that hydrogen war would be so suicidal that no government is likely voluntarily to embark upon it, and by the

[5] Article by Quincy Wright, professor emeritus of international law at University of Chicago. *Foreign Policy Bulletin,* published by Foreign Policy Association-World Affairs Center. 36:85-7. F. 15, '57. Reprinted by permission.

rise of independent nationalism above ideologies, evidenced by "Titoism" in Yugoslavia, by the developments in Poland and Hungary, and by declarations of the Soviet Union, Communist China, and the United States in the autumn of 1956.

This trend toward decentralization and internal restraints in the great alliance systems and toward the reduction of the international influence of ideologies presents new opportunities for the United Nations. This was illustrated by the initiative that the Security Council, the General Assembly and the Secretary-General were able to take to stop hostilities in the Middle East and to unite world opinion on the Hungarian episode in the autumn of 1956.

The General Assembly might discharge its function of "initiating studies and making recommendations for the purpose of promoting international cooperation" (Article 13) by examining the obstacles to cooperation arising from the development of ideological blocs, propagandas, and misunderstandings hostile to the peaceful coexistence of nations.

The General Assembly might also exercise supervision over regional arrangements and defense alliances to give assurance that their aims and practices are in conformity with the purposes and principles of the United Nations. While the Charter expressly requires that measures for collective self-defense and the activities of regional arrangements be reported to the Security Council (Articles 51, 54), it would seem that if the Security Council fails to function in this matter the General Assembly can and should exercise supervision by calling for reports and recommending modification of agreements to assure that they are in conformity with the Charter.

Progress in disarmament, admittance of neutralized states and universalization of United Nations membership would also be helpful.

(2) Identification of the United Nations with the National Interests of Its Members

The exclusive identification of most people with the symbols of a particular nation or a particular ideology and exaggerated ideas of sovereignty tend to create the view in some states that the United Nations is, or may be, hostile to national interests. This view overlooks the fact that the original members would not have ratified the Charter and nonmember states would not have struggled to be admitted unless national governments generally believed that a functioning United Nations is in their national interest, a belief frequently expressed by Presidents Truman and Eisenhower.

The United Nations might contribute to identifying itself with national interests by a more effective public relations program, by expanding technical assistance programs, and by more care in avoiding encroachment upon the domestic jurisdiction of members by consulting the World Court on this issue unless hostilities require immediate action.

(3) Peaceful Solution of International Controversies and Conflicts

Improvement of United Nations procedures to discharge this important function would strengthen the organization.

The events of the autumn of 1956 suggest that the initiative and diplomatic skill of the Secretary-General may be of great importance. The refusal of Hungary to admit Mr. Hammarskjöld raises the question of his right to diplomatic access to the governments of all members. Under the Charter the Secretary-General is the chief administrative officer of the organization and is entitled to bring political problems before the Security Council. By practice he is the representative authority to make agreements with states in the name of the United Nations. The International Court of Justice has defined the United Nations as an "international person" with some of the powers of a state under international law. Many of the members send permanent diplomatic representatives to the United Nations. These circumstances would seem to justify the Secretary-General in claiming diplomatic access to the governments of all members and in sending occasional, or perhaps permanent, diplomatic representatives to their capitals.

General Assembly recommendations have authorized a core of trained mediators available to states to assist them in the solution of controversies. Experience suggests that a single skilled mediator can contribute more to the pacific settlement of political controversies than a commission or committee composed of representatives of states. The latter are necessarily incapable of acting freely and rapidly in such a situation.

The General Assembly and Security Council might well revert to the League of Nations practice of assigning a *rapporteur* to formulate resolutions with the object of achieving consensus. The actual practice, by which partisans of one side seek to align the necessary majorities over the opposition of the other side, has tended to exaggerate cold-war considerations, has prevented the Security Council from functioning effectively, and in the General Assembly, has subordinated the peaceful solutions of disputes to ideological propaganda and voting victories.

General Assembly procedures should better integrate impartial fact-finding, advisory opinions of the Court, mediatorial action, and diplomatic initiatives of the Secretary-General, with a view to isolating the particular controversy from the degenerating influence of great-power rivalries, and to recommending a just and acceptable solution.

(4) Discouragement of Aggression

"To insure that armed force will not be used save in the common interest" is a major function of the United Nations. National decision-makers would be more likely to refrain from aggression and to unite against it if they knew exactly what constitutes aggression.

It seems clear that in the intent of the Charter, aggression refers to the use of armed force in international relations unjustified by defensive necessity, by invitation of the state in whose territory the force is used, or by authority of the United Nations itself. If this limited concept is accepted, it seems possible to work out a precise definition which attributes a use of armed force to a government, which distinguishes international from domestic uses, and which justifies international uses.

The procedure of first dealing with hostilities by provisional measures calling for cease-fire and withdrawal of force is contemplated by the Charter and has been generally followed by both the League of Nations and the United Nations. The obligations of members of the United Nations to observe such provisional measures whether by the Security Council or by the General Assembly might be clarified by supplementary agreements.

If such measures fail to stop hostilities, or even if they succeed, United Nations police action may be called for as it was in the autumn of 1956 in the Sinai Peninsula.

The Collective Measures Committee, established by the Uniting-for-Peace Resolution of 1950, proposed an earmarking of forces by members for such emergencies. The capacity of the United Nations to discourage aggression would be aided by a permanent police force—perhaps financially supported by a small percentage of the military budgets of all members—and by the more certain availability of earmarked contingents contributed by member states in emergencies.

The ability of the General Assembly to discourage aggression would be increased if a general treaty were negotiated, and open to ratification by all members, committing the parties to earmark contingents and to accept Assembly recommendations for a cease-fire, for determination of aggression and for utilizing such contingents. The Thomas-Douglas Resolution, introduced in the United States Senate in 1950, proposed such a supplementary agreement with a proviso that it would apply only if the General Assembly acted with a two-thirds majority including at least three of the principal powers.

Such an agreement would not only strengthen the United Nations directly but would reduce the need for such discriminatory and provocative special alliances as NATO, Warsaw, SEATO and the Baghdad Pact.

A UN POLICE FORCE? [6]

UNEF's [the United Nations Emergency Force's] extraordinary success [in preserving the peace along the Egyptian-

---

[6] From article by Robert C. Good, research associate of the Washington Center of Foreign Policy Research. *Commonweal.* 69:615-17. Mr. 13, '59. Reprinted by permission.

Israeli frontier] points directly to the question: why not make it permanent? Why not endow the UN with more than an "emergency" force dependent on year-to-year allocations from UN members, but a standing force ready, able, and willing to jump the next time a frontier catches fire? Isn't this, at last, the way to make the UN really "effective"?

For Americans especially this has seemed an attractive possibility. Shortly after UNEF was established, John Foster Dulles told the Senate Foreign Relations Committee: "I would be glad to see, myself, some more or less permanent character given to . . . the United Nations Emergency Force." United World Federalists, always trying new keys in the lock which bars the way to "world order under law," eagerly grasped the UN peace force idea. . . . President Eisenhower . . . said . . . [that events] demonstrated "the need for such a force in being."

Months ago it became known that the Secretary-General's staff was preparing a thorough survey of the UNEF experience complete with recommendations for the future; many concluded that the hour to strike for a permanent peace force had come. But when Mr. Hammarskjöld's report was released, it contained relative to a standing force neither prescription, nor blueprint, nor even a modest hint that such a force might be a good idea. Instead, he said, that it would be "without great practical value and certainly would not warrant the substantial sacrifices involved."

The high hopes of so many collapsed because these hopes had been based on two misunderstandings, the first relating to the nature of UNEF and the second to the nature of the UN itself.

UNEF, contrary to much popular opinion, did not by military intervention create peace in 1956, and does not by military force keep the peace today. It is not an army nor perhaps even a police force in the full sense of either term. The fighting stopped in 1956 as a result of pressures which were brought to bear on Britain, France, and Israel largely outside the UN—the pressure of the British Commonwealth countries; the stern disapproval of the United States; and the threat of the Soviet Union to turn a regional conflict into a world-wide crisis. UNEF, explained the Secretary-General in his summary report, "is in no sense a military force exercising, through force of arms, even temporary control over the territory in which it is stationed."

Misunderstandings concerning UNEF are compounded when the nature of the UN itself is not clearly understood. The UN is not easy to understand partly because the present organization bears no real relationship to the blueprint drawn at San Francisco in 1945. . . .

The enormous transition in the peace-enforcement function of the UN from the blueprint of 1945 to UNEF of 1956 may be set forth in a single, but not-so-simple, sentence: while the UN Charter provided for the enforcement of peace through the concerted action principally of the great powers whose consent alone was necessary to such action, UNEF by definition is limited to small powers, and depends not only on the consent of two-thirds of the voting members of the General Assembly, but upon the explicit consent of the host country and at least the implicit consent of *all* the parties to the dispute!

Because UNEF is a small force (it has never exceeded six thousand) made up of contingents from small nations (no other formula would have been acceptable), it cannot establish or maintain itself against organized military resistance. Because UNEF is the instrument of the General Assembly, a body with no constitutional authority to coerce, it cannot force consent to its operation; its operation must presuppose consent. Egypt's Dr. Mahmoud Fawze labored this point at UNEF's founding: "Our clear understanding . . . is that this force is in Egypt . . . to help Egypt, with Egypt's consent."

What then is UNEF? It is a tool, a device, for making less volatile any situation in which the disputants mutually desire to reduce the likelihood of violence. As one knowledgeable observer suggested, "Its role is merely one of assuring that what everyone wants to happen does happen." It is not an international army; it is an international burglar alarm. If triggered by attacks from one side or the other, the alarm will ring in the General Assembly. Its authority in the first instance is not the authority of force, but the authority of prestige—the prestige of those members of the Assembly whose affirmative vote brought UNEF into existence to begin with. "Its sole purpose," summarized Mr. Hammarskjöld, "was to maintain quiet and prevent the recurrence of incidents." This is a modest role, but an extremely useful one. Why then, did the Secretary-General "veto" the effort to make UNEF a permanent UN fixture, a standing force, available for immediate use in some future crisis?

Several reasons have been proffered by Mr. Hammarskjöld. Though the UNEF experience was instructive it was also unique. The circumstances which made its deployment possible during the Suez debacle were not likely to be duplicated, as the crises . . . [during the summer of 1958] in Lebanon and Jordan illustrated. A "UNEF" in Lebanon would have become embroiled in the internal conflicts of the nationals of the country since the situation took on the aspect of civil, rather than international, hostilities. A highly trained and mobile group of UN observers, however, was used to good advantage. For its part, Jordan would not hear of a UN force for fear it would joggle rather than stabilize her already unsteady position. Of course the Secretary-General did not rule out the possibility of future situations arising in which a UN force would again be useful. But he did emphasize that each situation probably would be distinctive enough to demand a tailor-made force, with skills, matériel and personnel all cut to the peculiar specifications of the situation once it arose.

Another problem was that of financing. Though its usefulness in stabilizing the Egyptian-Israeli frontier has been fully demonstrated, UNEF moves from one financial crisis to another. How much more difficult would it be to finance by voluntary contributions a similar force permanently organized, trained, equipped, ready to go—but who knows when and where?

The many technical difficulties clearly identified in the Secretary-General's report reflected perhaps an underlying political difficulty which could not be publicly identified—the fear of some states that this child of their ingenuity would somehow emerge like Frankenstein's monster to overwhelm its parent.

The response to UNEF has, in fact, been ambivalent. No one but the Communist bloc denies its usefulness; but many small states are uneasy concerning the precedent it represents. In the vote . . . [in November 1958] which extended UNEF's life for another year, seventeen small nations abstained, including all the Arab countries. India, while faithfully if not enthusiastically supporting UNEF, had serious reservations about its establishment during those hectic days in early November 1956. These reservations India has now transferred to the permanent force idea which it finds both "impractical" and "fraught with danger" and to which it therefore stands "irrevocably opposed."

There are strong emotional overtones to this attitude which India's Krishna Menon did not try to conceal from the General Assembly.

We could not consent to the taking of troops to the soil of other countries, even though they are United Nations troops—they are still foreign troops. It may be that some delegations may regard this as an excess of nationalism, but the experience of foreign troops on the soil of our land is too fresh for us to forget.

Beneath the overtones of emotion are the undertones of political concern. The Communists express it crudely, but some Asian states think they discover a kernel of truth within the husks of Communist propaganda. Once the imperialist powers had established a permanent UN force, said the Communist delegate from Bulgaria, 'it would not be difficult for others deliberately to create such an atmosphere that the governments of the smaller countries would be compelled to have United Nations troops on their territory." Though everyone agrees with Mr. Hammarskjöld that a UN force must not be "used so as to prejudge the solution of the controversial questions involved," some fear that the very existence of a standing force would make it difficult to resist its deployment, and once deployed the force might be used as a lever to help alter the status quo.

In this connection it is significant that Pakistan has urged the establishment of a permanent force while India has resisted it. The explanation is Kashmir, concerning which sentiment in the UN has been running strongly in favor of Pakistan's position. Pakistan no doubt hopes, while India fears, that a permanent force might evolve into an instrument which indeed would be used "so as to prejudge the solution of the controversial questions involved." Both the fear and the hope may be ill-founded. But as long as they exist on the part of members anxious to enlist or resist the UN's involvement in efforts to change the status quo, the permanent peace force is likely to remain only an idea.

Sensing the political climate and fully aware of the technical difficulties involved, the Secretary-General is strongly opposed to pressing for a permanent force at this time. But he has said that his office might well keep "the situation under constant review" and he has suggested that it might be useful to "take soundings" to determine which governments would be willing to contribute forces and under what circumstances. This should certainly be done for it would be a great pity if unpleasant realities were to cancel the future possibility, in appropriate circumstances, of turning again to the UNEF device.

WHAT THE UNITED STATES SHOULD DO [7]

The isolationism of the 1920's which kept the United States from participating in Woodrow Wilson's plan to avoid resort to World War II is still alive. If unchecked, it may contribute to the onslaught of World War III, which few of us would survive. . . .

It is possible to mention a few of the things the United States can do to further its interests, which are identical with the prevention of war.

[7] Press-release extracts from address by Philip C. Jessup, Hamilton Fish Professor of International Law at Columbia University and former U.S. delegate to the UN, at annual meeting of Conference Group of U.S. National Organizations on the United Nations, New York City, May 4, 1960. Carnegie Endowment for International Peace. New York. '60. Reprinted by permission.

Failure on our part to make clear an awareness of the true interests of the United States resulted recently in the defeat of the effort [to repeal the Connally Reservation—see "The Connally Reservation," in Section IV, below] to have us make effective use of the World Court. A comparable sluggishness may enable the same blind forces to defeat approval of the Antarctic Treaty [for free use of the continent for peaceful scientific purposes; for freezing of all territorial claims and banning of all military activities in the area—Ed.]

New States

The United States should favor structural changes in the United Nations to deal with the huge increase of membership and especially the African states which have recently, or soon will, become members. Pending the long slow process of amendment of the Charter, the United States should now support a change in the distribution of seats in the principal organs. Eastern Europe is represented by the Soviet Union and the extra seat in the Security Council claimed for that area should go to an African state. In alternate years one of the two seats now usually allocated to Latin America and to Western Europe should be made available for an Asian or Middle Eastern state.

In the composition of the many special committees and commissions which are established every year, the United States should see that Asian, African, and Middle Eastern states have adequate representation.

Blocs

Some persons seem to think that voting blocs in the General Assembly of the UN are bad. Actually they are a normal development in any legislative or deliberative body, like the Congress or the state legislature in the United States. The United States should not hesitate to deal with the blocs, but there is no need for it to try to form or maintain a bloc of its own like a NATO bloc. Blocs are especially useful in elections when a seat on some body is assigned to a region; the states in the region ought to caucus and indicate to other states which of their number they put forward as a candidate. . . .

Specific ways in which the United States could further give support to the whole United Nations system include:

1. The United States should ratify the general treaty concerning the privileges and immunities of the UN. We have so far refused because we insist on collecting a few dollars as income tax on salaries of American citizens employed by the UN.

2. [Make] greater use of UN in place of bilateral channels especially in technical assistance and in the use of the International Atomic Energy Agency. Present trends are encouraging.

3. Amend the United Nations Participation Act which was passed by Congress in 1946. It now provides that the President of the United States is authorized to apply economic sanctions against an aggressor when called upon by the Security Council. It should be amended to give him the same authority if, in case of a veto in the Security Council, the resolution is passed by nine votes or if, under the Acheson Uniting for Peace Resolution, it is passed by a three-fourths majority in the General Assembly.

4. Support international cooperative effort, through UN channels or through the scientific societies as in the successful model of the International Geophysical Year, to make rapidly available to the continent of Africa all possible advantages of science and technology.
   Examples: Perfecting cheaper methods of desalting sea water to make the oceans available for irrigating the Sahara desert areas; use of TV transmitters by hovering satellites for aid to education in relatively inaccessible interior districts.

5. On the political front start negotiating with Allies, with India, the United Arab Republic and other Asian, Afri-

can, and Middle Eastern states to find a generally accept-able solution for the China problem. Such a solution might cover these points among others:

a. The people on Taiwan cannot be abandoned to the untender mercies of Peiping.

b. Technical complexities of seating delegates to the UN must be met.

c. The reality of the mainland situation would be ac-knowledged as it was even by Mr. Dulles.

d. Peiping would get the seats in the UN while simul-taneously Taiwan (Formosa) would be admitted as a separate member of the UN.

e. The people of Taiwan would be offered a free plebi-scite under UN supervision in which they could choose:

    i. Independence to continue as a separate state, member of UN;

    ii. Rejoin Japan;

    iii. UN trusteeship, indefinitely or for a term of years, with the UN itself (as authorized by Article 81 of the Charter) as trustee or any other trustee selected by the General Assembly; or

    iv. Join the mainland under Peiping.

f. The General Assembly would adopt a resolution which "calls upon" all members of the United Na-tions to support whatever solution was adopted; under this resolution, alone or with other states, the United States could maintain a collective self-defense pact with Taiwan.

6. Repeal the Connally Reservation and make more use of the World Court, encouraging like-minded states to join us in a "law bloc" which would always be open for others to join.

To accomplish much of this program we would need to eliminate in this country some of those excesses of nationalistic fervor which we tend to deplore when they are evidenced in the newly emerging states.

THE UN BETWEEN EAST AND WEST [8]

Can the UN, by its diplomatic activities, be the instrument of, can it at least facilitate, an easing of tension in relations between the Communist and non-Communist blocs?

This is essential if security is to be organized through the cooperation of the big powers and not in conflict with, or even in spite of, one or two of them. Another way of putting the question is: If the UN has failed as an agency for collective security in the military sense, because of this division among the great powers, can it increase security and strengthen peace by its activities in the international diplomatic field aimed at removing this division? The answer *should* be "Yes."

The UN *should* be effective in this way through both its formal and less formal activities; through its provision of a world stage and, even more important, through its work done behind the scenes on that stage.

Experience has shown both the limitations and the value of the UN as an international agency for the discussion and negotiation of international problems. As a world organization, neutral and objective in its operation, it has advantages possessed by no other international agency. It can bring international opinion, the international conscience, to bear on any given problem with maximum impact in a way which is not possible elsewhere. It can influence diplomatic negotiations by doing so.

Public discussion at the UN of international problems prior to negotiation—or as a part of negotiation—has, of course, not always been productive of good results. The technique of public international discussion, at the UN and elsewhere, can be used to becloud issues and frustrate negotiations. But there have been occasions when discussions at the UN have made subsequent agreement easier. If there are not more of these occasions, that is the fault of governments, not of the UN.

Nor should its failures be allowed to conceal the present and, even more, the potential value of this body as a world

[8] From "What Future for the United Nations?" by Lester B. Pearson, Nobel Peace Prize winner, Canadian ambassador to the United Nations, 1948-1956, president of the General Assembly, 1952. New York *Times Magazine*. p 14+. S. 27, '59. Reprinted by permission.

diplomatic assembly. In the UN, governments have to parade, not only words, but policies, before the scrutiny, friendly and unfriendly, of the international public. This important function of clarification, of analysis, of education, is taking place every day that there is a UN meeting anywhere in the world.

This process can . . . be abused. Such abuse occurs when governments drag tense and explosive situations before an international assembly, not for the purpose of finding solutions, but for justifying national policies or for attacking someone else. When this is done, in highly publicized and bad-tempered debate, it is the worst possible prelude to negotiation and settlement. But it need not be done that way.

Unfortunately, it is this destructive political and propaganda activity at the UN that gets the most publicity; the acid and acrimonious debate aimed, not at assisting the search for a solution, but at establishing one's own innocence and the other side's guilt if that search fails. Debate of this kind lends itself to dramatization and exaggeration by those who are reporting it for public consumption. Conflict is always headline news. It needs no publicity agent. Peaceful and constructive achievement, however, often has no one to sing its praises.

The experience of recent Assemblies indicates that the UN is becoming more and more the vehicle for this kind of political activity. Up to a point, its use for these purposes is inevitable and need not cause any great anxiety. But when this use constitutes the chief value of the organization for a growing number of its members, then its value for genuine, constructive diplomatic discussion and negotiation is prejudiced and may be destroyed. It becomes merely an instrument for the promotion of national policy and not one for international agreement.

If this trend goes too far, the result could be fatal for any substantial political and diplomatic achievement by the organization. For this development, the Communist members must take the major share of the blame, but not all of it.

There is another danger to the future of the UN which should be faced. It is the tendency to bypass it completely; to search for solutions by negotiations outside its walls; to ignore its existence in such a search, whether the problems are political, economic or social.

There are many problems, of course, for which the normal processes—or even abnormal processes—of diplomacy are best designed. The UN was never meant to replace those processes, especially in relations between the big powers. That is true. But if it is ignored or bypassed in matters which affect *all* of its members, then it will soon cease to be an effective agency for international discussion or negotiation—or, indeed, for anything else.

It will become merely a platform for propaganda and polemics; one from which the leaders of states can be sure of a large audience and of maximum coverage when they visit the United States for other purposes.

If all the big decisions are to be made at conferences and meetings—whether on summits or slopes or on the level— which are outside the aegis or influence of the UN, and the Secretary-General, as the voice of the world organization, is not even consulted, then the UN as an influence on political and diplomatic development will wither away.

There is another field in which the UN can and should play an increasingly important part; in which, indeed, it already has important achievements to its credit.

I refer to its work in social, economic, and humanitarian fields, directly or through its affiliated technical agencies. The importance of this work is often obscured by more controversial and less constructive political and diplomatic activities.

Nothing, for instance, could be much more important, in the promotion of stability and security in the world, than the provision of international, technical and capital assistance to materially underdeveloped countries. The UN should be the machinery through which this work is conducted. But political considerations have once again often frustrated something that was very much in the minds of those who drew up the Charter. As a result, this kind of international action, assistance to underdeveloped countries, has become more and more a matter of bilateral, or of limited group arrangements. If this trend continues, then the importance of the UN in this field, where it could do so much, will also be lessened.

In short, the results which could be achieved by the world organization in the fields of diplomacy, economic assistance, and social progress will depend on the policies and practices of the member governments; on their desire to use the UN to the maximum possible extent for all genuinely international purposes.

If they do not have this desire, and if they do not base their policies on it, then the world organization will gradually lose its value as an effective piece of international machinery. It is strictly up to the national governments, especially those with greatest power and influence. *They* will decide the fate of the organization. . . . Perhaps the lead in preventing . . . [a] decline should come from that responsible group of middle powers who have as much at stake in securing the peace as the big powers but whose policies are not determined by "imperial" interests or world-wide commitments.

NO ALTERNATIVE TO UN [9]

The fact is that there is no practicable alternative to the United Nations. Escapist solutions simply do not meet the hard reality. This is so whether the escape be toward the unifying vision of world government or, on the other extreme, toward fragmentation into the dozens of ill-defined arrangements to which we are now party. The supreme advantage of NATO, which makes it one of the few exceptions, is its limitation to a fairly precise military task. It is true that military cooperation cannot be carried on in a vacuum of political understanding. Nevertheless, . . . such an understanding cannot be developed through only one diplomatic forum. The fallacy is not merely overemphasis of the political potential of NATO. It is the undervaluation of the UN.

This is not to say that the United Nations is a panacea, nor even that it is adequate to its objective. No one would

[9] From "N.A.T.O. and the U.N." by Ernest A. Gross. *New Leader.* 41: 12-16. Ja. 27, '58. Reprinted by permission.

contend that the United Nations can work *perfectly*. But it is quite a different thing to say that it can work *better*.

In this context, there is no need to urge large improvement in the uses of the United Nations in the fields of economic cooperation and development of human rights. This necessity is only too obvious.

The reasons usually advanced to support the contention that the United Nations is "undependable" apply for the most part to the major political issues which either confront or divide the free world. Soviet abuse of the veto does indeed make the Security Council undependable. Even more, it is dangerous as an instrument of diplomacy for any matters in which the Soviets can use the veto power with mischievous intent. Nevertheless, the General Assembly and other UN bodies are not veto-bound, because they take action under majority rule.

Then, it is said, the newly elected members of the Afro-Asian group make the General Assembly undependable, if not downright irresponsible. Experience thus far justifies the conclusion that, with sustained United States leadership, the new membership does not undermine or corrode sound policies. In certain issues, existing majorities are increased. In others, it might be more difficult to get a majority, but this works as an element for stability quite as much as for obstruction. Moreover, recommendations of the Assembly which are vague, or which do not command wide voting support, do not generate much compulsive quality.

The coalition of freedom must expand in order to survive, since freedom is the natural condition of man. Yet freedom requires clearly understood goals and practicable means to advance toward them. These must be supplied by leaders who inspire, in order to out-do drivers who coerce. Given such leadership, the United Nations—even if its membership be as large as the planet—will always rally to the call of freedom.

III. NATO AT THE CROSSROADS

EDITOR'S INTRODUCTION

The United States is the pivotal member in a global system of defense alliances embracing a third of the world's area and population. The key element in this system is the North Atlantic Treaty Organization extending from North America through Western Europe eastward to Turkey. (Other regional pacts: the Rio Treaty in the Western Hemisphere, the Central Treaty Organization in the Middle East, and the Southeast Asia Treaty Organization. Additional bilateral treaties bind the United States defensively to Taiwan, South Korea, Japan, and other nations.)

The first two articles, by Admiral W. F. Boone, USN, and Sir Charles Webster, commemorate NATO's tenth anniversary with differing appraisals of its unique character as well as its achievements and shortcomings. They merely hint that all is not well within the Alliance. Indeed, as with other mainstays of American foreign policy, NATO has in recent years come under severe questioning—on military, political, and economic grounds.

Militarily, the debate has centered on NATO's strategy as embodied in the twin concepts of Sword and Shield. So intricately involved is this debate—resting as it does, among other variable factors, on the new weapons technology and the resulting vulnerability of this country to enemy attack, a reevaluation of Soviet aims in Western Europe, and mounting assertions of nationalistic independence on the part of our Allies and ourselves —that discussion at higher levels takes on the aspects of a game of three-dimensional chess.

The major points are set out with unusual clarity by Michael Howard in a BBC talk here reproduced, which reflects the views of America's top NATO specialists. Barring an East-West agreement for the control of nuclear weapons, concludes Howard, "there seems no choice for the nations of Europe except between relying increasingly on independent national deterrents or pooling their nuclear resources and with them much of their status as sovereign powers."

Dismissing the first of these alternatives as guaranteed to wreck the Alliance, Alastair Buchan develops the idea of a new NATO High Authority to control missile and other nuclear-weapons systems on a regional basis.   Both in this and in the next selection, in which he elaborates the concept of "Interdependence," Buchan takes pains to emphasize that, however great the need for cooperation and consultation within the Alliance, a political federation of its members is neither required nor desirable: "It would be a dubious step because an international government might be considerably less efficient and flexible . . . than a number of national governments working on an agreed plan."

On the political plane, the question at bottom is leadership. Can it, should it emanate from the United States alone, or from the celebrated postwar combination of America and Britain, or from a triumvirate of America, Britain, and France, on which General de Gaulle has been so forcefully insistent? Drew Middleton's article, though written prior to the surprise cold snap from Moscow in May and the quick closing of NATO ranks that it produced, remains essentially sound for it illustrates a recurrent fact: NATO is united when Russia is hostile to the West, disunited when Russia is friendly. The marked fissures in Western policy, now obscured by the need to present a united front against an obstreperous Khrushchev, will surely reappear in one form or another when East-West tensions again relax.

Besides demanding a decisive role for his country in the guidance of NATO affairs, particularly with regard to the use of nuclear weapons, General de Gaulle claims that Russia's and China's outflanking maneuvers make NATO's restricted vigil over its own parish obsolete. What is needed now, he says through his spokesman Maurice Schumann, is a global strategy—coordination by the Western Big Three of their policies in "the unprotected parts of the world."

With certain reservations this viewpoint is shared by NATO's Secretary-General Paul-Henri Spaak: "It may well be that Europe will no longer be the main scene of the long-term struggle between communism and the free world. This will very largely take place in the economically underdeveloped countries of Africa and Asia."

Economically, then, according to Spaak, "the essential need of our time will be for the free world to unify its economic policy, to pool its resources and to organize the rational conservation and distribution of its wealth."

And what, finally, of NATO as a purely military organization? John Fischer, tying several familiar threads together, comes up with an unorthodox proposal which is nonetheless appealing to informed circles here and abroad.

NATO— KEYSTONE OF DEFENSE [1]

NATO is the keystone of the supporting arch of United States foreign policy. . . . The Alliance is in accord with the principles of the United Nations Charter, Article 51 of which recognizes the right of nations to enter into agreements for collective self-defense. By exerting a powerful influence for peace, NATO makes a vital contribution to the aims of the United Nations. There is, however, no organizational link between the two.

NATO came into being when events following World War II revealed the aggressive, expansionist policies of Soviet Russia. The seizure of Czechoslovakia and the Berlin blockade [in 1948] were the clinchers. The Soviet objective of world domination could only be countered through a collective effort. . . .

The North Atlantic Treaty was signed in Washington on April 4, 1949. Belgium, Canada, Denmark, France, Iceland, Italy, Luxembourg, the Netherlands, Norway, Portugal, the United Kingdom, and the United States were the twelve original

[1] From article by Admiral W. F. Boone, USN. *United States Naval Institute Proceedings.* 85:22-43. Ap. '59. Reprinted by permission; Copyright 1959 by United States Naval Institute.

signatories. Through subsequent protocols, Greece and Turkey became members on February 18, 1952, and the Federal Republic of Germany joined on May 5, 1955.

The treaty sets forth objectives in the political, cultural, and economic fields, but, common defense is fundamental to the concept and development of NATO. The genesis of the military organization and activity of NATO is found in Article 5 of the treaty, which states in part: "The Parties agree that an armed attack against one or more of them in Europe or North America shall be considered an attack against them all. . . ."

History has known many alliances forged under the stress of war, but a coalition such as NATO is unprecedented in time of peace. Never before in peacetime have nations placed their forces under the over-all command of foreign officers. Never before have so many nations signed a treaty to consider an attack on one an attack on all. This is the core that binds the NATO nations together.

Is NATO a powerful influence for peace? Do we get more security for our money by pooling our defense effort with Canada and the free nations of Europe, by allotting some of our defense expenditures to foreign military aid, by joining our NATO partners in an Allied military command structure? Are U.S. security interests better served by deploying U.S. forces along Allied forward defensive lines—land, sea, and air—in Europe than by playing a lone hand under a "Fortress America" concept? The answer to all of these questions must certainly be "yes."

The unprecedented vitality of this coalition in time of peace is all the more astounding in view of the technological revolution of the last decade. When the Alliance was formed, the United States had an atomic monopoly, and except for atomic bombs in the possession of the United States, the munitions and weapon delivery capabilities of the armed forces of the world were essentially those of World War II. The intervening ten years have seen the development of thermonuclear weapons, the rise of Russia as a nuclear power, the arrival of the missile age, the nuclear submarine, and the exploration of outer space. Yet

NATO is more effective than ever in achieving its basic purpose. It is the prime factor in U.S. policy toward Europe. The evolution of NATO strategy has kept pace with the revolution in military technology. . . .

When General Eisenhower was appointed in 1950 to be the first Supreme Allied Commander in Europe, he had at his disposal less than twenty divisions. The equivalent divisions which now would be available to General Norstad in continental Europe on D-Day, or a few days thereafter, represent a numerical increase by a factor of nearly four. He now would have over 6,000 aircraft, mostly jets, compared to about 400 available in 1950. It is difficult to cite meaningful figures as to naval vessels, but the naval forces which are now tabled for NATO are about eight times as large as in the beginning. Today, many NATO forces in Europe have a tactical atomic delivery capability.

IRBM's [intermediate-range ballistic missiles] and other surface-to-surface missiles are now operational in Europe. At their meeting in December, 1957, the NATO heads of government decided to establish stocks of nuclear warheads to be readily available for the defense of the Alliance in case of need. Anti-aircraft missiles are in place on the Continent and ready.

But even with a generous factor of calculated risk cranked in, the Alliance does not yet have all of the forces which, in the best military judgment, are required to provide an adequate defense against aggression. However, minimum force levels have now been fairly well recognized and accepted by the member governments.

The NATO supporting structure has been vastly strengthened. In 1950, there were fifteen airfields available to NATO in Europe. Today there are several hundred ready for use. . . . In the past seven years, tens of thousands of miles of cables and land lines, and countless radio links, have been added. There are now several thousand miles of NATO pipelines in service where there were none in 1950.

In 1950, NATO nations expended some twenty billion dollars for defense; in 1957, the same nations spent about 56 billion security dollars. Some two billions have been expended on common . . . projects, including war headquarters, naval bases, and maritime airfields as well as others previously mentioned. Progress is being made toward the integration of transportation systems and logistic support.

Hand in hand with these numerical and material gains, there has been a steady improvement in the quality of NATO forces, so that there is now a much greater readiness, cohesiveness, and combat capability than in the early years of the Alliance. NATO commanders and supporting staffs all down the line know their jobs and, within the limits of resources provided, are fully prepared to go into action. Plans have been refined, tested, and rehearsed in many NATO training exercises, large-scale and small.

Best of all, the NATO partners are learning to understand and trust each other and to work smoothly and effectively together.

All this is progress. But progress in NATO is meaningful only as it is measured against the constantly increasing military capability of the Soviet bloc. Military posture is purely a relative thing. The threat which brought NATO into being still exists. . . .

NATO *is* working. It is working so well that the dissolution of the Alliance has become a prime political objective of the Kremlin. What better proof is needed that NATO is a success?

THE RECORD TO DATE [2]

On April 4, 1949, the representatives of twelve states signed at Washington the instrument which brought into existence the North Atlantic Treaty Organization. . . . NATO . . . had two purposes. It was meant to be a means by which its members could coordinate and combine their political and economic policy. But it had also a more immediate purpose—to provide the basis for the defense of Western Europe from aggression by the Soviet Union, and events made it necessary for the

[2] From "NATO's Tenth Birthday," reprint of British Broadcasting Company talk by Sir Charles Webster, British historian. *Listener.* 61:620-1. Ap. 9, '59. Reprinted by permission.

organization of common defense to become its urgent and almost exclusive preoccupation.

As a defense organization NATO is certainly a unique experiment. Fifteen states now belong to it, some of them far from the Atlantic, voluntarily joined together for the common defense of their independence and democratic institutions. For this purpose they have set up an organization such as has never before existed in time of peace. There is an international army in Europe, directed by a supreme commander with an international staff, and provided with an infrastructure of oil pipelines, depots, airfields and missile sites, built by a common effort and extending from the long perimeter which separates the NATO countries from the Eastern bloc right up to the Atlantic Ocean. Its equipment now includes tactical nuclear weapons and intermediate ballistic missiles, together with the latest jet fighters and anti-tank guns. There is also an international fleet under another supreme commander. Both are directed politically by a council of ministers of the fifteen countries, who have officials to represent them in their absence. Strategic direction has been placed largely in the hands of a standing group of representatives of the American, British, and French chiefs of staff. Behind all these are ranged the hydrogen bomb, the strategic air forces of the United States and Britain, and the intercontinental missile.

How far has the absence of war in Europe been due to the existence of NATO? Some think that it was only the hydrogen bomb that preserved the peace; but this is to simplify the situation too much. In 1949 Europe was so badly organized for defense that a limited but sudden effort by the Soviet bloc might have had an immediate success. What NATO has done is to organize Western defense in such a way that to penetrate it the Soviet Union would have to make extensive preparations and consciously determine to engage in a major war. It is a shield which cannot be beaten down without a great and determined effort by its adversaries.

Moreover, through NATO another extraordinary transformation has taken place in Western Europe—the reconciliation of

France with Germany—or at least with the Federal German Republic. For many years various proposals were put forward by which Germany could be rearmed without renewing the danger she had caused in the past. It is certain that without NATO no such means could have been found. Now her forces are to be so closely integrated . . . that this danger has been almost completely removed. At the same time Federal Germany has recovered her independent status and dignity. NATO has not only reduced the fear of attack from the East; it has also reduced the fear of a resurgent and aggressive Germany.

But NATO has had much less success in its wider objectives. It has not enabled the Atlantic Community to obtain a common political and economic policy. Its continental members have been preoccupied with their own economic integration, which was indeed partly due to their desire to counter the economic preponderance of the United States. Moreover, worldwide organizations exist for economic coordination. Thus little has been done to implement Article 2 of the treaty concerning economic collaboration which was intended to be an important part of it.

Nor was NATO a convenient center for the integration of political actions. There could be no supreme commander in politics. Thus the United States and Britain tended to form a common policy before the other NATO countries were consulted. Recently, however, this situation has been changing. France has demanded the same equality of position in the direction of political action as she already possesses, at any rate in theory, in the standing committee on defense. Political problems have been more and more remitted to the NATO permanent council of deputies in Paris before decisions have been made, instead of afterwards. . . .

But it would be a mistake to think that NATO has not grave defects or that it has yet reached its final form. NATO has more than a hundred committees and subcommittees engaged in working out its problems—far too many, most people believe. Even in the age of the jet airplane, it is a great handicap to have its permanent defense committee stationed in Washington and its permanent political committee in Paris. Nor can ministerial direction be given as often and as quickly as is necessary, while the official deputies cannot take decisions on fundamental points.

Not only the machinery but the whole strategy of NATO has been criticized. There is in some quarters a vain desire to put back the clock and transform Germany into a neutral zone— a policy often described by the misleading word "disengagement." But such a transformation could come about only if a world-wide reduction of armaments were to take place, and that still seems far away. Some people also have been shocked at the arming of NATO with nuclear weapons and missiles. They are afraid that Europe might become the theater of an atomic war while the rest of the world escaped. But this is impossible; if such weapons were used it would only be as the prelude to an all-out hydrogen bomb war. They are in fact part of the great deterrent.

Finally, and perhaps most important of all, NATO is the means by which the United States shows by the presence of her armed forces on European soil her determination to stand or fall with Western Europe. Without that assurance Western Europe could not obtain the unity, courage, and organization to defend itself. When it can do so without the aid of the United States we shall have passed into a different age. Meanwhile NATO is the sheet anchor not only of the defense of Western Europe but of all the free world. Though present discussions may well cause considerable modifications to be made both in its machinery and in its strategy, it is still indispensable to enable the free and democratic nations to resist the massive totalitarian power wielded by a handful of men in the Kremlin.

THE MILITARY EQUATION [3]

Anxiety has been increasing, over the past year, in both Europe and America, about the whole military situation of the

[3] From "America and the Defence of Europe," reprint of British Broadcasting Company talk by Michael Howard, political affairs writer, delivered as a review of *NATO and American Security*, edited by Klaus Knorr, and published by Princeton University Press, 1959. *Listener.* 62:1139-41. D. 31, '59. Reprinted by permission.

West. . . . The reasons for this disquiet are discussed in an interesting, if not easily readable, symposium by some of America's leading defense analysts which the Princeton University Press has recently published under the title *NATO and American Security*. The contributors adopt many different approaches and their arguments do not always agree; but broadly speaking their conclusions are these.

For the past five years, ever since it became obvious that the NATO powers could not or would not raise the 100-odd divisions which had at first been thought necessary to defend Europe, NATO strategy has rested on the concept known as the Sword and the Shield. In the event of a Russian attack, the ground forces in Europe were not to fight a prolonged campaign, but to act as a Shield to hold up the onslaught for a limited period, while the Sword of American air power struck at Russian bases and cities, from airfields scattered around the perimeter of the Eurasian land-mass as well as from the United States. Without the Shield, the Sword could not be brought into action, for there might be no clear *casus belli* [cause of war]; without the Sword, the Shield forces could impose—so it was thought—so brief a delay that it seemed barely worth undertaking the defense of Europe at all.

This idea was never immune from criticism. The decision to equip NATO forces with tactical atomic weapons, and the declared intention to use them even if the Russians launched a purely conventional attack, awoke particular misgivings—especially when military exercises made it clear that the use of such weapons would kill over a million German civilians and injure several million more. But it has not been developments *within* NATO that have caused doubts to grow so remarkably during the past few months, but developments outside, affecting the Sword rather than the Shield. The original plan assumed a considerable margin of superiority on the part of the American striking forces over the Russian. For at least five years it has been accepted that the Russians have the capacity to strike at the homeland of the United States; but it has been assumed that their attack could be kept within tolerable proportions, partly by the counterforce capacity of the United States Strategic Air Command, partly by the wide dispersal of American bases which the Soviet Air Force would have to destroy if their own homeland was to escape unacceptable damage, and partly by the air defenses of the United States themselves. . . . The preponderance of nuclear power in American hands seemed so overwhelming that the basis of NATO planning appeared on balance to be perfectly sound.

During the last year or so all this has been changed. It has become obvious not only to military specialists but to the whole world that Soviet missile development has far outdistanced the West; and there is every reason to suppose that this lead is one not only in the development of missiles but in their production as well. The Russians, that is, not only have better missiles than the Americans, but they have considerably more. NATO planners have therefore to face the prospect not only that any American attempt to draw the Sword in defense of Europe would lead to devastating and inescapable retaliation on the United States but that the American Strategic Air Command, dependent as it still is on manned bombers flying from large and vulnerable bases, might be prevented by a Russian preemptive strike from ever getting the Sword out of its scabbard. For if the Russians know that any attack on Western Europe would provoke a certain counterattack by American bombers against Russia, they would naturally attempt to destroy those bombers before they attacked Europe at all.

Period of Readjustment

This position of inferiority is admittedly temporary. At present the Strategic Air Command attempts by wide dispersal and early warnings to reduce to a minimum the probability of any surprise attack achieving complete success. Within a few years it will have at its disposal enough "hard-based" missiles—that is, either housed in protected subterranean sites or mounted on mobile carriers—to make it impossible for any surprise attack to succeed at all. But until that day arrives not only the Americans but the people of Western Europe are faced with a delicate and dangerous period of readjustment; and what form that re-adjustment should take is becoming the subject of keen debate.

The first problem which forces itself upon us concerns the nature of the Shield. If the United States were no longer to intervene to turn any Russian attack on Europe into a global thermonuclear war, the Europeans must either be capable of repelling the attack, or acquire for themselves the capacity to retaliate against the Russian homeland which the Americans would no longer provide. In any case it is highly desirable to provide a stronger Shield: one that is more likely on its own to deter aggression. Can this be obtained by multiplying tactical atomic weapons? The Princeton experts are doubtful. The provision of these weapons to NATO forces has been justified on several grounds. One is that the West cannot match Russian manpower —an argument which is untenable in terms of statistics, whatever it may be in terms of politics. Another is that even though both sides are now equipped with nuclear weapons, on balance they favor the defense; but this a matter on which military specialists are far from unanimous. A third is that by ensuring that any Russian attack triggers off an atomic war we increase the deterrent to that attack; but since the possibility of keeping such a war limited to the battlefield is generally discounted by official circles on both sides of the Iron Curtain, and since in an *un*-limited atomic war the Russians would at present enjoy a preponderant advantage, the credibility of this deterrent, which amounts to a willingness on the part of the West to commit suicide, is extremely doubtful.

Deterring Attack with Conventional Weapons

For all these reasons a great deal of expert opinion on both sides of the Atlantic is coming round to the conclusion that an increase in forces armed solely with conventional weapons, which we would have no hesitation about using, will be a far more efficient means of deterring an attack on Europe than reliance on atomic weapons whose use will precipitate a holocaust from which we would emerge, if emerge we did, very much second best.

To produce such forces would be a matter of political rather than of military will-power. They need not be very large. The belief is spreading that with adequate mobility, a high standard of training and weapons improved by a diligent program of scientific research, a conventional force little larger than the thirty divisions at which NATO now aims might, if supported by adequate trained reserves, provide a defense for Europe at least as convincing as the present posture, and far less dangerous to the future prospects of mankind. A reserve tactical atomic capacity would still be needed to deter the enemy from using his own tactical atomic weapons and to retaliate if he did; but such conventional forces should be capable of performing all the functions for which the troops of NATO are at present organized: to deal with frontier incidents, to distinguish between local probes and deliberate sustained attack, and to fight for long enough to present the aggressor with the choice of abandoning his objectives or achieving them only by a total war in which the use of nuclear weapons could no longer be avoided.

The Princeton experts are almost unanimous in their belief that such forces would provide a tougher, because a more credible, Shield than does the screen of nuclear-armed troops which at present—in theory at least—holds the line in Western Europe. If they are right, no political or economic sacrifice . . . would be too great for us to attain it. But we would still need a Sword, if only to deter an aggressor from threatening us with his own nuclear capacity. Conventional forces may be the most credible and therefore the best deterrent to aggression, but their credibility depends on the existence, in the background, of a nuclear capacity to hold in check that of the other side. If the nuclear capacity of the United States will no longer suffice for this, then Europe must provide its own. It might, of course, seek the hazardous refuge of neutrality—but it would be a neutrality resembling rather that of Belgium, that hapless strategic highway between contending adversaries, than that of Switzerland, a state which has always reinforced its considerable geographical advantages by unstinting expenditure on weapons, by universal military service, and by the ceaseless study of war.

Sharp Differences Among Experts

On how Europe could provide this nuclear capacity the experts differ sharply. The difficulty that faces the United States will confront the countries of Europe as well. What country will go to the aid of any other when the consequence—not the risk, but the certain consequence—will be its own annihilation; when the question is not one of fighting for an ally but of dying with him? In logic the only answer seems to lie in every state being provided with, or developing, its own nuclear capacity: "hard-based" missiles, indestructible by enemy attack, and capable of inflicting certain and substantial damage on a larger enemy; guaranteeing even to the smallest state that large measure of immunity which the hornet derives from its sting. This is the logic which justifies the development of an independent atomic capacity by such powers as Britain and France, and which is likely to lead to a general dissemination of atomic weapons among the increasing number of powers with the scientific and technological capacity to make them.

Whether or no we can regard such a development with equanimity, the result for NATO can hardly be good. When each member relies primarily on its own deterrent for safety, obligations to allies will take a secondary place. The cost of such weapons can be met only by increasing defense expenditure, which requires high political courage when the international skies seem clear, or by saving on conventional forces; which have a strong claim, as we have seen, not to be reduced but to be increased. Already it is the nuclear, or near-nuclear, powers in Europe that find most difficulty in meeting their commitments in conventional forces. If European membership of the nuclear club increased, the task of the NATO authorities is likely to become impossibly difficult; and it is hard to see how the Alliance could be saved from disintegrating into a group of independent nuclear powers, each concerned principally with looking after itself.

The alternative is that NATO should develop its own common deterrent: a nuclear capacity to which all member-nations should contribute, which should be sited as strategic considerations might require—in British submarines, in Italian or Norwegian mountains, on French or German railway-trucks—and be subject, as are the conventional forces contributed by NATO members, to the authority of the Supreme Allied Commander. The strategic and economic advantages of such an arrangement speak for themselves; but so do the administrative and political difficulties. To the officials who have grappled with the problem of, for example, persuading all member-states of NATO to adopt a standard type of small-arms ammunition, the project will appear as Utopian as that of immediate and universal disarmament. The existing regime in France has refused its cooperation to far less ambitious projects, while to the British it would appear as an abdication of that sovereignty which alone enables us to retain our Commonwealth links. Yet the idea is gaining currency, and we may expect it soon to become the subject of widespread debate.

Whatever may be the decisions taken in the near future about Western defense, it seems clear that an era has ended—an era when the principal decisions about the defense of Europe were taken in Washington; and, as the Princeton volume shows, nobody realizes this more clearly, or is prepared to state it more frankly, than the Americans themselves. We may within the next few years see the United States and the Russians reaching, and enforcing, a world agreement for the control of nuclear weapons; but if this does not happen, there seems no choice for the nations of Europe except between relying increasingly on independent national deterrents, or pooling their nuclear resources and with them much of their status as sovereign powers. NATO, in short, is likely to play either a much greater or a much smaller part in our lives than it does today.

THE CASE FOR A NATO DETERRENT[4]

What must be designed, produced, and located in Europe is an IRBM [intermediate-range ballistic missile] designed for

[4] From "Wanted: A European Deterrent," by Alastair Buchan, British journalist and NATO expert. *The Reporter.* 21:28-30. O. 15, '59. © 1959 by The Reporter Magazine Company. Reprinted by permission.

the purpose—so that as the strategic equation between the United States and the Soviet Union becomes more stable and unbreakable from the mid-1960's, Europe itself need have no fear that it is a vulnerable no man's land outside the sphere of American protection.

If this is one of the principal strategic requirements of the 1960's, how is it to be met? Who is to finance a European deterrent? Who is to design it? Who is to control it? For America to hand out Polaris or other missiles to its European Allies, with no form of control, would be fatal. Within a month after Germany or Turkey had received theirs, the Scandinavian members—and probably Britain as well—would be out of the Alliance.

There are two broad alternatives: the formation of a European strategic deterrent with American encouragement, or the formation of a NATO deterrent under a new form of NATO authority.

The idea of two separate systems of deterrence in NATO—one North American and one European—has many attractions both for Europeans and Americans. It would satisfy the desire, so evident in France and Germany, to become less strategically dependent on the United States.; it would also satisfy the long-standing desire of American liberals for a strong and self-reliant Europe. But it suffers from some crippling defects. In the first place, the European Six—or even the Western European Union (the Six plus Britain)—does not comprise the whole of NATO in Europe, and to set up an integrated force based on either would cut across the whole command structure of NATO which it has taken so many years of patience to evolve. Moreover, it is very unlikely that Britain, given its strong feeling about its special relationship with Washington, would cut the transatlantic cable in the interests of such a dubious cross-Channel link. Finally, it is very doubtful if it would be strategically feasible for Western Europe to build a credible deterrent on its own in less than a decade, even with American encouragement.

The more realistic alternative of a system of deterrence in Europe under the control of NATO itself also involves a more adventurous leap into supranationalism. Such a program cannot be achieved on a basis of cooperation and unanimous agreement, which has been NATO's operating rule hitherto. It will require tough and unpopular decisions that Country "A" must have x number of missile sites for reasons of geography and terrain, while Country "B" has y—or none. It involves sorting out the competing views of firms, designers, and military staffs on fuel or guidance systems, designs, sites, control systems, and a hundred other problems which, if left to the process of ordinary negotiation, might take half a century to resolve. It cannot be done without American leadership and experience; yet the United States—its energies already taxed by the problems of intercontinental deterrence and with no direct national interest in an IRBM of the kind needed by Europe—cannot be expected to bear the whole load.

The speediest and surest way to meet these requirements is to set up a strong new authority in NATO—similar, on an Atlantic scale, to the high authorities that have been developed by the European Six. This does not necessarily involve turning NATO into any kind of federal system—which the NATO powers are, if anything, less ready to accept than they were a decade ago. It does not necessarily mean altering the role of the North Atlantic Council, that body of permanent ambassadors which is the highest day-to-day political authority in the Alliance, and which can take decisions only by unanimous consent. What now seems needed is the creation in parallel of a functional authority to deal with the missile, air-defense, and antisubmarine systems, serving a regional rather than a national purpose. Such an authority would have to operate on a system of weighted voting that would give power to the various countries according to their size or their contribution to the programs, and thus create a real incentive to nations like Britain and France to give it their fullest support.

THE MEANING OF INTERDEPENDENCE [5]

What interdependence has come to mean, at least to those who live at the heart of the Alliance, is this: that no NATO

[5] From "The Idea of Interdependence" in NATO in the 60's by Alastair Buchan, published for the Institute for Strategic Studies, London. Frederick A. Praeger. New York. '60. p 47-54. © 1960 by Alastair Buchan. Reprinted by permission.

country, including the United States, is now capable of assuring its own security. In other words, there is no longer such a thing as a national strategy even for the strongest powers in NATO, even though there may be many shades of difference in their foreign policies. Nor can they divide their policies into compartments, pursuing an allied strategy in Europe and a national policy elsewhere. The flexibility of Soviet power has now made a dual attitude of this kind impossible. . . .

In so far as Russia is genuinely capable of pursuing a more independent policy than the United States, it is because she is far less dependent on overseas trade and good will, because she can bring force to bear at many points of the compass without using the territory or communications of any other country, and above all because she has been prepared to sacrifice living standards to defense.

But the reasons why the Western Alliance must evolve a higher degree of interdependence than its Eastern counterpart go deeper than geography and trade. The expansion of Soviet military strength requires both a larger total effort—military, technological and economic—in order to maintain a stable balance of power at all levels. This in turn implies a greater degree of specialization among the different members of NATO. For only by such a differentiation of function can the superiority of the Soviet Union in many fields be adequately countered and the inevitable wastefulness—inherent in any alliance—be overcome. Moreover, a division of labor between the different members of the Alliance is rendered essential by the steadily rising cost and complexity of weapons.

It is important to be clear on one point. The loss of independence of action is not the same thing as an abrogation of sovereignty. The demonstration of events, from Suez to the Luniks, that the NATO powers must draw closer together, has produced much heart-searching among thoughtful people, and a revival of interest in Atlantic Federation. Most people would agree that such a federation is politically impossible and would be a dubious gain in strength and flexibility if it were possible. It is a forlorn hope, because a federation of democracies requires a legislature that is directly elected by the peoples of the federated area. In the mood of national self-consciousness which the economic regeneration of recent years has brought about, this is very unlikely to be acceptable to the existing legislature of any NATO country. It would be a dubious step because an international government might be considerably less efficient and flexible—particularly at the administrative level—than a number of national governments working on an agreed plan. The analogy of the foundation of the United States of America is quite misleading in this respect, because is was created at a time when central governments had miniscule responsibilities by comparison with today.

What emerges from any attempt to apply the concept of interdependence to the next ten years of NATO is not a blueprint for new institutions . . . but guiding principles in four areas of policy.

(i) Strategic Planning

. . . It is one thing to make speeches about the importance for the NATO countries of subordinating individual national interests to the general interest of the Alliance. It is quite another to translate this into terms of tanks, fighters and aircraft carriers. It is harder in military planning than in, say, economic cooperation, for there is a traditional connection . . . between certain kinds of military power and the pride or self-esteem of the nation itself. If some future review of NATO force requirements were to conclude that there was no longer a valid operational function for the U.S. Marines, the Brigade of Guards or the Chasseurs Alpins, one can imagine how likely it is that such a decision would be implemented by the United States, Britain or France. . . .

But the important point is that, given the limited total military resources which are available in NATO to confront the flexibility of Soviet power, a country's influence within the Alliance must henceforth be more closely related than hitherto to the extent to which its military power conforms to the over-all needs of NATO. If the argument that has been widely used, first in Britain and then in France, that it is necessary to have a complete array of military power in order to be influential . . .

persists, it will in the end produce six or eight separate nuclear weapon programs within the Alliance, all overlapping, some of dubious military value and all carrying great political dangers. Nor is it merely a question of nuclear weapons. It is an open question whether the navies of the smaller NATO powers serve a purpose commensurate with their cost. A more effective specialization of functions is not merely a matter of getting a more objective approach by ministers and chiefs of staff when negotiating changes in force requirements. . . . It is also a matter of political leaders educating their own public opinion to an understanding of what collective, as opposed to national, defense involves.

The corollary to this is that there must be a far more intensive system of consultation, and a much more profound level of agreement, about the needs of the future among the NATO powers. Twice-yearly meetings of foreign ministers and chiefs of staff, and one SHAPE exercise a year, are not adequate for this purpose. Too often a glowing communiqué at the ministerial level conceals a complete lack of agreement among officials, or at the levels of government where NATO decisions must be translated into terms of national policy. . . .

The crucial question of future priorities, of the balance between nuclear and conventional forces, between the needs of deterrence and the likelihood of limited war, problems of subversion and other ambiguous threats, would seem to require a major and continuous review by both ministers and officials, rather than a series of *ad hoc* national debates of the kind that have been taking place sporadically in the United States, in Britain, in France and in Canada, during the last two years. . . .

One difficulty has always been the limitation on the power of the United States government—owing to the requirements of American legislation—to discuss with her allies strategic concepts, let alone national plans, which involve the use of nuclear weapons. In practice, this has meant that over much of the recent past it has been difficult for American representatives to discuss or explain the problems of maintaining an effective policy of nuclear deterrence, and in consequence the ideas of some European governments are woefully out of date.

At the moment, Britain is the only country to whose representatives American officials can talk with full candor—a fact of which France is fully aware. And though the 1958 amendment to the MacMahon Act dealing with exchange of information gives a certain measure of discretion to the administration, Britain—because she has an effective delivery capability as well as nuclear bombs themselves—can be treated in a way in which France cannot, even after the Sahara explosion has taken place. . . .

There are signs that the U.S. administration has realized the extent to which the [MacMahon] Act [restricting transmittal of nuclear weapons data to other countries] is a direct incentive to smaller powers to develop their own nuclear weapon industry, and that it is taking steps to mitigate this situation, partly by making information on nuclear weapons more readily available to its NATO Allies, and partly by closer political consultation with them. But there is a great deal of leeway to be made up for the short-sighted views that have prevailed in Washington throughout most of NATO's first decade—in Congress, in the Pentagon, and in the Atomic Energy Commission.

(ii) Political Consultation

This growing diffusion of power implies a greater, not a lesser, obligation on the NATO powers to consult in advance of action on problems affecting not only the NATO area but the whole world. As the world grows smaller, so any ideas of spheres of influence become less tenable, even though it may become no easier for an Italian or Belgian minister to see the problems of the North Pacific through American eyes, or for an American or Danish official to see African problems through French or British eyes. If one danger of war arises from the expansion of a local conflict into a limited war, and from a limited war on upwards, a fracas in Algeria or Quemoy or Nairobi is something which affects countries far from the scene of action. In this sense, General de Gaulle's request to Washington last October for a general review of the world situation on the part of the United States, France, and Britain, was a legitimate one—though his refusal to participate in many vital aspects of European defense unless France is given access to, and a virtual veto on, American decisions on the use of force anywhere in the world, was not.

It is the very fact that most of the NATO powers have wide and various interests outside the Alliance, which makes this principle of consultation in advance of action so important. It would be a source of weakness rather than of strength if NATO were to become a monolithic bloc, whose members were always expected to act in exact concert at the UN, in Africa, or in Asia. It is the breadth and diversity of Western contacts with the rest of the world which gives the Atlantic Community much of its moral and political strength. . . . The only alternative to insisting that no action is taken by any member anywhere in the world without the unanimous agreement of, say, the Atlantic Council—an arrangement which might break up the Alliance— is to insist on the principle of regular though informal consultation in advance of action.

To this rule there must, for the foreseeable future, be one exception. In the very unlikely, but conceivable event of a Soviet surprise attack against Europe or the United States or both, mounted without any warning whatsoever, the President of the United States and SACEUR [Supreme Allied Commander Europe] would be defaulting in their obligations to their Allies if they did not take immediate action—even if it meant no consultation with their Allies whatever. Of this the Russians must be in no doubt.

(iii) Diplomatic Negotiation

Closely linked with the principle of consultation is that of negotiation. It has become fashionable to suggest that the United States and Russia would make greater headway in negotiations on nuclear tests, disengagement or disarmament, if they could talk *tête-à-tête* without being "compassed about with so great a cloud of witnesses" in the shape of their smaller Allies. Much of the European nervousness at the prospect of Summit conferences has derived from a fear that both Moscow and Washington may believe this to be true, though there is no evidence to show that it is.

But true or not, such an approach cannot be reconciled with the idea of interdependence within NATO. This may prove to be a drawback, but it cannot be avoided. NATO is by no means an ideal alliance: it is very far from being "one equal temper of heroic hearts": it comprises states of very different historical backgrounds, of very unequal levels of wealth, skill and wisdom. But for better or worse it is the only transatlantic alliance that has ever been created in time of peace, and it is at present the most effective that can be achieved. Therefore the larger powers within it cannot at one moment accept the benefits it brings them, and at another disregard it in order to talk with Moscow the more sophisticated dialect common to great powers. The point is that the strength of the larger powers in NATO at the conference table is directly related to the degree of cohesion and fundamental agreement that exists within the Alliance as a whole.

(iv) Specialization

It has always been easy to draw up a theoretical scheme for a more rational and intelligent division of effort within NATO on manpower and production than exists today. On a purely financial calculation it is absurd for the United States and Canada to maintain forces of their present size in Europe—the Canadian brigade in Westphalia costs as much to maintain as two European divisions. The additional manpower for the defense of Europe might more rationally be drawn from those nations where there is still considerable underemployment. Similarly, naval construction for the Alliance should be concentrated in European yards where ships can be built more efficiently and more cheaply than in the United States. On the other hand the production of aircraft, missiles and electronic equipment should be concentrated in North America, where the size of the industries concerned makes for flexibility and speed of production.

But it is unrealistic to proceed too far with arguments of this kind, for one knows that they have no chance of being implemented. The United States cannot entirely abandon the ground defense of Europe to the Europeans because ordinary people throughout Europe would take this as a sure sign of her effective withdrawal from the Alliance. Equally important is the fact that defense production and research is intimately interrelated with national economic and employment policies. Moreover, the difficulty of reconciling national interests in the field of defense production becomes greater the higher the proportion of the national resources that is spent on it. With defense expenditure absorbing anything between a quarter and more than a half of national budgets, defense production has become inextricably involved with commercial and employment policies. . . .

Nevertheless, a better rationalization of effort there must be, if NATO is to meet the requirements of the next decade without the imposition of heavy new burdens on the public which, even if it were politically possible to meet them, would in themselves aggravate international tension.

THE QUESTION OF LEADERSHIP: UNITED STATES [6]

Perhaps the most important and certainly the least advertised problem set the Western Alliance by the change in relations with the Soviet Union is whether the United States will be able to lead the West in the new conditions of the 1960's. . . .

The ability of the Western powers to meet the politico-diplomatic offensive of the Soviet Union and, simultaneously, to maintain NATO as the military base for an agreed diplomatic position . . . [are the key issues at stake].

Seldom has success seemed so distant. A gradual easing of relations with the Soviet Union, superficially at least, has weakened the resolution of some NATO members to support the Atlantic Alliance with the necessary men, money and material. Deep differences, rooted in national aspirations, separate the United States, the United Kingdom, France, and West

[6] From "If the U.S. Does Not Lead," by Drew Middleton, New York *Times* correspondent. New York *Times Magazine*. p 10, 79-81. D. 13, '59. Reprinted by permission.

Germany on the approach to the Soviet Union and the policies to be followed in . . . [dealings] with Premier Khrushchev.

To retain leadership of the Western world, the United States must solve two separate but related problems arising from the present situation. First, differences among the fifteen member nations of NATO must be composed. Second, a joint position of the Western Allies must be formulated.

The solution will not be easy. This is undoubtedly the most difficult problem of statesmanship, as opposed to salesmanship, that the Eisenhower Administration has faced since the end of the Korean war.

Differences over NATO have been aggravated among the smaller members of the Alliance by the gradual easing of Soviet military pressure. This has lessened NATO's immediate military importance to some of these governments. Other factors affect the attitude toward the Atlantic Alliance of Europe's Big Three, leading them to follow independent and at times contradictory policies.

These independent policies have clashed with the agreed Western approach in some international sectors, such as the character of NATO and with the policy of the United States in others. In settling these clashes among the United States' chief allies in Europe, the President will be dealing with a crisis of strength.

Obviously, it will prove impossible in practice to separate these two problems. The most parochial minor disputes between two NATO members affect the West's ability to present a united front to the Soviet Union. And some of the deepest differences among the British, French and Germans are over policies to be followed when President Eisenhower, Prime Minister Macmillan and President de Gaulle sit down at the council table with Mr. Khrushchev. . . .

The Atlantic Alliance has passed from its military stage to a period of politico-economic activity. Fear of military defeat bound the British, French, Americans and Italians together in 1917 and fostered the pattern of Anglo-American military partnership in 1941-1945. That fear is no longer an urgent factor in determining the policies of the European powers. Moreover, the fear of Soviet military aggression, which in the circumstances meant defeat, that helped create NATO in 1949 is rapidly vanishing.

Nor can American statesmen count on economic dependence to make the Allied leaders more amenable to United States policy. The man in the street in Duesseldorf, Lyons or Coventry believes his present prosperity is due pretty much to his own efforts. Officials in the chancelleries may think differently. But they have to take the man in the street into account when framing policies.

How can the United States solve these problems in this atmosphere?

The first and most important step appears to be a clear definition of the international aims of the United States and of the means the United States proposes to attain these aims. A second and related step would be a detailed explanation of the thinking that has led to the formulation of these aims and the adoption of these means.

A third step is to explain again, clearly and definitely, that the enormous political, economic, and military strength of the United States cannot be exerted in the interests of the Western Alliance if the people of the United States, who are the majority of stockholders in that Alliance, perceive that foreign policies initiated and supported by their government are to be watered down or gutted for reasons that to them seem narrowly nationalist. . . .

If the United States definitely explains the aims of its policy and the reasoning that lies behind these aims, this could unite the Western powers in NATO and provide the basis for agreement on the policies to be followed in the talks with the Soviet Union.

But precision is vital. This diplomatic task cannot be achieved by public demonstrations of friendship, no matter how fervent, or by back-slapping, no matter how eminent the backs.

The time has come to state exactly where we stand in this new situation in the world. For example, the statesmen and

officials in Washington and London are convinced that the
time has come, because of changes in the internal situation in
Russia and because of the mutual deterrence exercised by nuclear
weapons, to negotiate seriously with the Soviet Union on the
chief issues that endanger the peace.

This conviction has alarmed the French and the West
Germans, particularly when it is equated with the negotiation
of an interim status for West Berlin, because they believe that
any negotiation over Berlin's status would be bad negotiation.
General de Gaulle and Dr. Adenauer believe, quite rightly, that
negotiation involves concessions by both sides if agreement is
to be reached. They also believe that any concession the West
might make to the Soviet Union on the Berlin question would
weaken the whole Western position in Germany.

This argument has been put with a good deal of force
and clarity by the French President and the German Chancellor.
The counter-argument has never been so put by the United
States.

The American argument is the basic explanation for the
change in the American and British attitude toward negotiations with the Soviet Union. Briefly the argument runs that
improvement in the economic conditions of the Russian people,
increases in their standards of education and information and
the effect upon the Russians themselves of an end of continued
foreign crises—a condition maintained almost without a break
from the end of the revolution in 1917 until 1958—will fundamentally alter the Soviet Government's approach to world
problems.

But the argument has not been made. If the West is to
take the initiative in the long period of diplomatic negotiation
that lies ahead, the argument must be made successfully to
Dr. Adenauer and General de Gaulle or they will continue to
resist any change from the familiar formulas of the cold war.

This argument is the basis on which United States policy
will rest in any series of negotiations with the Soviet Union.
It must be accepted by America's Allies or they will continue to
make the mistake of thinking that we are dealing with the

same sort of Soviet policy that has waged the cold war. For the West to talk in those terms now, as Dr. Adenauer frequently does, is deemed folly. Mr. Khrushchev is far too wily not to take advantage of an Alliance that talks in 1960 with the accents of 1950.

The argument against negotiation over West Berlin takes on a different complexion when the basis on which American thinking rests is explained. But hand in hand with this explanation there must be a clear definition of American aims in the negotiations. No one is thinking of abandoning Berlin. No one is going to engage in a "give-away" program with the Soviet Union. What apparently is intended and what must be spelled out is a series of negotiations, infinitely protracted, directed at achieving the means of getting along in the world with the Russians. This means negotiation not only on Berlin and Germany, but also upon disarmament, the economic and political problems raised in the development of the new nations of Africa and Asia, among which communism is perhaps the most important political problem for the West, and the long-term issue of dealing with Communist China.

None of these issues is going to be settled quickly or easily. They will never be settled unless a start is made by a united Western world.

The blunt facts are that the United States is the foremost power in the Western world. Decisive military, economic, and political power resides in Washington, not in Paris, Bonn or London. Beyond the Elbe lies a powerful Russian empire that has decided to use political and economic ends to secure its aims, but which still commands an immense military power that only the United States can balance.

The penalties to the Western world of failing to recognize these facts and shaping policies in accord with them are obvious and terrible.

A division of Western Europe into a rabble of ill-armed nationalisms only invites Soviet diplomacy to make the individual offers of treaties and pacts that have always been in the background of Russian policy. If a single European country wishes to pursue a purely nationalist policy in its relations with the Soviet Union, no one will be better pleased than Mr. Khrushchev.

The Soviet Premier fears, and there is every reason why he should fear, a Western world united behind a clearly defined policy. But he does not fear individual Western governments or their leaders, unless the latter speak to him on behalf of a generally agreed Western policy. . . . The Soviet Union can be stopped by realistic negotiation over outstanding issues by a united Western coalition led by an American government that not only knows exactly where it is going, but has stated its direction and its reasons so clearly that there can be no doubts or divergencies among its Allies.

THE QUESTION OF LEADERSHIP: FRANCE [7]

If General de Gaulle's intentions with respect to the Atlantic Alliance are worrying you, let me give you a bit of good advice: question Nikita Khrushchev after his talks with the President of the French Republic and you will be fully reassured. . . .

In September 1958, three months after assuming power, the General sent a memorandum to Washington and London on the necessity of adapting the Atlantic Alliance to the changes that had occurred in the world since 1949. This text was neither made public nor kept entirely secret. So it necessarily led to erroneous interpretations that could have been avoided if someone had taken the trouble to explain the objectives of this French initiative. But it is still not entirely too late to provide such an explanation.

As the first example, anyone unfamiliar with this memorandum of September 1958 cannot understand why General de Gaulle decided to restore independence to the French Mediterranean Fleet in the event of war. Previously this fleet had been committed to go under the Allied Atlantic Command

[7] From "What the West Doesn't Understand About de Gaulle," by Maurice Schumann, chairman of the Foreign Affairs Committee of the French National Assembly. *Réalités in America.* 113:58-63. Ap. '60. Reprinted by permission.

Britain and France—coordinate their policies in the unprotected parts of the world, and that zones to which the North Atlantic Treaty does not now apply be divided into organized theaters of operation.

The General goes even further. To encourage the development, and thus the strengthening, of the Western Alliance, he has set an unprecedented example. On September 16, 1959, he declared—while admitting the risks involved in his daring proposal—that French policy on the Algerian problem was to be based on the principle of self-determination. Even before September 16 he had conveyed his intentions by word of mouth to President Eisenhower, who replied: "I do not see how a democratic country can refuse to help you from now on."

This way of going about things clearly meant that the President of the French Republic, in order to ensure effective cooperation in Africa by the Western powers, was ready to set up a system of permanent consultation among the Allies. If he had intended to impose his own will and to demand unconditional support, he would not have started by confiding in the President of the United States. But you cannot ask a statesman to be only half-way logical.

De Gaulle showed he was ready to accept the sacrifices implied in a common policy and common strategy south of the Mediterranean, but in the same spirit he drew his conclusions from the fact that no such common policy and strategy exist today. His decision on the fleet was a warning which meant: "In wartime, a military force must carry out the war's objective. The Western powers must define, both for Africa and for Europe, objectives which can be adopted by all in the West. If the Western powers cannot do this, each nation must preserve its own military forces to defend its own interests. This decision should not, however, keep us from coming to an agreement. For it is more than likely that we can and will discover that our essential interests are, in the finaly analysis, not divergent but identical. Surely the best way to avoid a great danger is to see it coming when it is still a long way off.". . .

However, this explanation of the French position would seem more satisfying if there had been no other differences. It is not enough to justify the refusal to allow the Atlantic Command to install missile bases on French soil or to set up atomic and hydrogen weapons, a decision the more grave since it compelled the Supreme Commander of NATO, General Norstad, to transfer American fighter-bomber bases to the territory of other NATO members. . . .

But the memorandum of September 1958 goes further, or rather puts the difficulty on another plane: it asks that any use of nuclear weapons—which, whatever the place or the circumstances, would mean a risk of total destruction for all—be a matter for joint decision. This controversial point is the least understood of all those which have caused Franco-American misunderstanding. But, as we shall see, it is by no means the least dangerous.

Everyone, and most of all Mr. Khrushchev, knows that if any one of the members of NATO is a direct victim of atomic aggression, the Supreme Headquarters will automatically strike back with the same weapons. Everyone, beginning with Mr. Khrushchev, knows that, since the decision taken by the Atlantic Council in 1954, if any country belonging to NATO were the victim of a "classic" aggression (that is, with nonatomic weapons), the West, to make up for the great superiority in manpower enjoyed by the aggressor, would use tactical atomic weapons. These hypotheses leave room for almost no margin of doubt.

But what would happen, on the other hand, if war broke out over some matter outside the zone defined by the Atlantic Treaty? It always comes back to this question. To imagine such an event, one has only to recall what transpired in November 1956. The French and British had landed at Port Said without consulting the United States. At once, Marshal Bulganin threatened atomic reprisals on London and Paris. Events then continued as if Washington had at that time let it be known that the United States would determine its attitude in sovereign independence, and that it could not consider itself as automatically committed, since the territories of its Allies were exposed to destruction by the consequence of an action undertaken without the assent of the United States.

From a political point of view this attitude could perhaps be criticized. But legally it was irrefutable. It is evident, however, that if things should happen in the same way again, communism would again be the beneficiary and the arbiter of the discord dividing the West against itself. According to de Gaulle there is only one way to keep this fatal crisis from developing sooner or later: at the highest level a list must be drawn up, and kept up to date, of the potential causes of war. There must be a jointly approved policy laid down for every eventuality with agreed tactics and strategy to eliminate any chance of misunderstanding, for this is the real danger. . . .

No one can reproach the French government . . . for wanting to be associated with the initial decision [to use nuclear weapons] which, even if it deals with the Middle East or the Straits of Formosa, can entail as a consequence the annihilation of France by H-bombs.

Said, not without reason, the average American in November, 1956: "Nobody asked my advice before starting an operation against Egypt even if the operation is justified. Now I see that the U.S.S.R. is threatening to go to Nasser's rescue. I have no intention of being dragged by a sort of automatic process into a war my country did not decide on." De Gaulle reasons just the same way when he says: "If a country like France must ever make war, the war must be her *own* war." This formula, clarified by its context, means: A conflict started at almost any point on the globe can—if the alliance between Communist China and Russia comes into play for example—quickly become a world war; defense of the free world may require that France run a risk of total destruction. She accepts this risk as long as the decisive choices are not made without her participation. The danger will diminish, moreover, insofar as everyone knows exactly what the situation is. In other words, the atomic warheads will be welcome in France as soon as the French government—as representative of a world power and delegate of the free countries of Western Europe—is, along with the British government, associated with the management of the atomic strategy of the West. But this demand would be unreasonable if the country which formulated it did not contribute as much as it could to the over-all strength of the free world. That is why General de Gaulle has not for a moment thought of going back on his decision, made some ten years ago and maintained by all the governments of the Fourth Republic, whether presided over by Antoine Pinay, Pierre Mendès-France or Guy Mollet, to bring France into the "atomic club."

I have heard it said that the reason for this decision was to make France independent of the United States and to facilitate the setting up of a sort of "third force." Such an interpretation is not only insulting but absurd. We know perfectly well that our atomic possibilities will never allow us to compete with the two "giants." And even if we were able, we should not have the slightest desire to do so. General de Gaulle's atomic policy—strictly the same on this point as that of the Fourth Republic—hinges on two propositions. First we must fulfill the necessary conditions so we can benefit from the MacMahon Law governing the granting of American atomic aid, and strengthen the Franco-American alliance, within the framework of NATO, by an atomic collaboration that would make our countries more tightly associated than ever. Secondly, we must add our efforts to those being made by the United States and Great Britain to persuade the U.S.S.R. to accept international control of atomic weapons. This would deliver the world from its nightmare and allow the industrial powers to divert to under-developed countries an increasing proportion of the billions now used for the manufacture of death-dealing weapons. . . .

POLITICAL AND ECONOMIC POLICIES [8]

Those who believe in the utility and effectiveness of the Atlantic Alliance must ask themselves whether, in spite of its undeniable success, NATO, as constituted today, adequately

[8] From "The Political Future of NATO," by Paul-Henri Spaak, Secretary-General of NATO. NATO Letter. 7:1-7. D. '59. Reprinted by permission.

meets the Communist threat in the new form it has assumed. I fear that the answer must be negative. For, although the Atlantic Alliance has achieved its main aim, and is therefore very definitely a success, the Communist threat has spread both geographically and ideologically. It is no longer a threat confined to Europe. It is at least as great a danger to Asia and Africa, while, at the present time, it is probably economic and social rather than military and political. . . .

Provided that the military forces in the free world are maintained efficient and up to date, it may well be that Europe will no longer be the main scene of the long-term struggle between communism and the free world. This will very largely take place in the economically underdeveloped countries of Africa and Asia. . . .

The Atlantic organization has built up a satisfactory military apparatus and is, we hope and believe, strong enough to discourage any aggression. We must now seek to give the Alliance the solid foundation of a united, or at least a coordinated, foreign policy. Armed force, after all, is an instrument of policy. It is not much use having the instrument if you have no policy.

In the second half of the twentieth century a purely military alliance is not enough. Certainly, we have to explain to our peoples that they might one day have to defend themselves in common against a common enemy; but we have also to explain to them that they must learn to live together. Somehow they must grow to understand what solid and permanent interests they have in common.

The authors of the Washington Treaty understood this very well, but during the first six years of its life the Alliance concentrated mainly on the military effort.

At the beginning of 1956 the foreign ministers of member countries invited three of their number to study the political aspects of the Alliance and to make a report, and the Suez crisis in that year gave dramatic evidence of the urgency of finding a solution to this problem.

For in this matter of grave international policy, the French and the British took one position and the Americans took another, which was closer to that taken by the Russians.

It was perfectly clear at that time that such a situation, if it were to occur again, would be fatal to the Alliance, and everyone was therefore in a suitable frame of mind to accept the report which the three ministers produced at the end of the year.

Political Consultation

For this report vigorously underlined the absolute need for coordination of foreign policy and recommended that there should be methodical consultation amongst the Allies before any individual action was taken. . . .

It is certainly no easy matter to coordinate the foreign policy of these countries. I would not like to say that all our efforts have been successful, but I can say that we have achieved substantial results. It is a new experiment and we shall not be able to decide finally upon its success or failure for a number of years. Generally speaking, the consultation has been well applied in regard to relations between East and West. For two years almost all the notes exchanged between the great powers of the Alliance and the Soviet Union were seriously examined and discussed beforehand in the Permanent Council. It can, therefore, be said that these notes were the expression of a concerted common policy and not merely of the ideas of one or other member country. . . .

The encouraging fact is that whenever it has been a question of meeting the Soviet Union in negotiations, differences on the Western side have always been surmounted. . . .

But . . . the organization is threatened with a difficult problem in regard to political consultation.

Some governments think that the Atlantic Alliance, which is a limited regional defense pact, is insufficient today. They point out that, in its present form and with its present functions, it cannot provide a solution to problems lying outside its geographical limits. They maintain that NATO neglects the vital problem of global strategy.

Governments who feel this way have a tendency to treat consultation within NATO as of secondary importance and this is certainly harmful to our organization. I consider that we must find a remedy for this because I believe there is a real case for the argument that NATO's procedures are out-of-date.

It is not possible in 1959 to isolate European problems from those of Africa or Asia. In the first place, the Communist pressure is more and more directed towards those two continents. Secondly, certain members of NATO have wide and important interests outside the territory covered by the Washington Treaty.

What should we do? We cannot change the treaty. We cannot ask the member countries as a whole to extend their military commitments. But we can make the general consultation in NATO more systematic and thorough, and we can add to it a system of limited consultation in which those countries would take part which have special interest in the problems in different parts of the world.

In these restricted consultations all the political, economic, and military problems should be studied with the purpose of reaching a coordinated policy. It should be more than a mere exchange of information and documents. It should lead to the conclusion of particular agreements.

There may be some difficulties about this system, but I see many advantages. The most powerful members of the Alliance, who would, of course, be members of all the restricted committees, would thus acquire a general view of world problems and would be in a position to coordinate the action of the Alliance. This, it seems to me, would be a step towards the elaboration of a global strategy.

The countries with limited interests would have the opportunity to concert their action with their more powerful Allies and would no doubt obtain from them the help they need. Finally, the other members of the Alliance would not be kept in the dark. On the contrary, they would be informed, to the extent that they were interested. . . .

We must be realistic about our own strength. I am not going to discuss . . . the relative merits of a liberal or planned economy. I would only draw your attention to one point. In the Communist world all economic forces without exception are at the disposal of the political objective. This is a formidable instrument. In the free world, on the other hand, competition within our countries and competition between our countries remains the rule. Such a system may possibly be suitable for dealing with the economic and social problems of Europe itself, but I am sure it is not capable of dealing with the world-wide problems such as the problem of underdeveloped countries.

For me, the essential need of our time will be for the free world to unify its economic policy, to pool its resources and to organize the rational conservation and distribution of its wealth. This will be an extremely difficult task. It is far easier to mobilize the forces of the West against a possible military aggression than to demand a coordinated economic policy. For economics are the last refuge of all selfish and nationalistic illusions. Our experience within NATO has been quite disappointing in this field, and enables us to see how great the difficulties are.

We have not yet achieved in NATO any real standardization of armaments. We have not been able, except once or twice on a very small scale, to share out the tasks in connection with new military production. We are constantly repeating in one country experiments already successfully carried out elsewhere. We persist in reinventing what has already been invented and we refuse to trust our friends with secrets already known to our enemies.

The advantages of individualism and the blessings of freedom are all very well, but when carried to such extremes of disorder and selfishness they hardly seem so desirable.

This sort of thing, as I have said, may still be just tolerable in our own highly prosperous countries. But it is certainly not tolerable for economically underdeveloped countries. Everybody can see that, for it is in the underdeveloped parts of the world that the decisive struggle between Communism and the free civilization will be decided.

Our own peoples, for many years to come will, no doubt, be proofed against Communist temptation. But let us not forget that we constitute a very small part of the world population. There are all the many millions of others who will tip the balance.

What should we conclude from all this? That NATO stands at the crossroads and that its effectiveness, and perhaps its very existence, depends upon its power of adaptation.

NATO is ten years old. For the first six years the principal effort was military. During the following four years it has been political. In the years to come the principal effort should be economic.

Please do not misunderstand me. It is not a question of destroying what already exists. We must preserve, consolidate, and improve what we have done.

There is no question of pushing military or political problems into the background. On the contrary, they must be even more closely attended to. Events may force us, and do force us, to concentrate our attention on the economic problems, but we can only handle these problems successfully behind the shelter of our defensive force, and so long as we hold together in the essential business of our relations with the Communist world.

MILITARY POLICY—A PROPOSAL [9]

Anyone who looks sharply can see that NATO's sword rests in a hand which can no longer wield it. As a result the Russians are maneuvering with a new confidence, and panicky whispers are beginning to run through our own ranks.

But the battle is not yet lost. We still have time—a little time—to face up to the fact that our old defender is gone, and to devise something to take the place of NATO's propped-up shell.

Some of the most thoughtful military men in this country and in Western Europe are reasonably hopeful that this can be done. Because their private views differ at many points from the official positions of their governments, they cannot be quoted. Without violating any confidences, however, I can say that what follows is based on many hours of conversation with men whom I believe to be well informed and in whose judgment I have

[9] From "The Editor's Easy Chair; the Corpse on Horseback," column by John Fischer, author and editor of *Harper's Magazine*. *Harper's Magazine*. 220: 14+. Mr. '60. Copyright © 1960, by Harper & Brothers. Reprinted from *Harper's Magazine* by permission of the author.

confidence. If the conclusions are sober ones, they are not (to me, at least) altogether discouraging. . . .

NATO was originally conceived as a tightly-integrated force of sixty divisions—seven of them American, the rest to be contributed by our Allies from Turkey to Scandinavia. With its accompanying air and naval units, this was deemed to be the minimum needed to offset the 175 Soviet divisions drawn up beyond the Iron Curtain, plus the sixty divisions of the Eastern European satellites.

Actually NATO never reached anything like its planned strength. On paper it musters forty-five divisions—but only twenty-one of these are on the crucial front from the North Sea to the Mediterranean, many of them are unready for combat, and a truly unified command has never been achieved. The explanation is simple: most of the European nations did not deliver the troops they had promised.

France alone had a plausible excuse; her armies were busy fighting colonial wars in Indo-China and later in North Africa. The others had no excuse they could mention publicly. But for most of the last decade the private reasoning—in Bonn, Brussels, Copenhagen, Rome, and many another capital—ran like this:

"NATO's real strength lies not in its land divisions, but in the American Strategic Air Command. What actually holds the Russians back is their fear that if they invade us, America will blot out their cities with nuclear bombs.

"So why should we go to the trouble and expense of raising the armies we promised? We can safely let the United States carry the main burden of defending Europe. All we need to do is to make sure that she keeps a few divisions on European soil—primarily as hostages. If these American soldiers are lost in the first Soviet attack, then we can be certain that U.S. bombers will strike back. Meanwhile, we can drag our feet—making a token contribution of men and money just big enough to keep the Americans from quitting in disgust."

To us this may sound cynical; most European politicians would have called it realism. After all they understood, better than American taxpayers possibly could, just how war-weary their people were, how shaky their economies, how weak their governments. The strain of building new armies in the early years of the cold war might well have ripped apart the damaged fabric of their societies. . . . Moreover, at the time, their calculations (however cynical) were accurate; their strategy worked—so long as the United States had a clear lead over the Soviets in both nuclear weapons and the means of delivering them on target.

As the last decade drew to its close, however, that lead dwindled—and then shifted, abruptly and dramatically, to the other side. For the Russians proved, by a whole series of demonstration shots into outer space, that they could destroy our cities just as easily as we could destroy theirs. Indeed, easier —since their missiles soar on engines twice as powerful as anything we have, and a lot more of them stand ready on combat launching pads. If they can hit the moon (as we, at this writing, cannot), who doubts that they could hit Chicago? [10]

So the line of argument in the privacy of European government offices began to shift, in accordance with the new situation, to something like this:

"No matter what the State Department says, can we really count on the Americans any longer? Will they actually go to war with nuclear weapons in order to save Berlin—or, for that matter, Paris or Athens? That just doesn't sound rational. No nation governed by sane men is likely to commit suicide for the sake of a distant ally. And suicide is precisely what it would be, since the Americans themselves calculate that they would lose 40 per cent of their population and 60 per cent of their industry in the first hours of such a war.

[10] Alarming as it is, the Russian lead in nuclear missiles is not quite catastrophic. The best estimates I can get indicate that until about 1963 they will be able to hit us harder than we can hit them—but still not hard enough to tempt them into starting a war. Unless they can count on knocking out virtually all of our strategic bombers and missiles in their first attack, we could still strike back hard enough to make the gamble unattractive.
   The number of missiles required for such a knockout blow varies from day to day—depending on the number of weapons we have ready to go, how widely they are dispersed, and how well they are protected. Today, for example, they might need three missiles to be sure of killing one of ours on the ground; a little later, when we complete "hardened" underground launching sites, they might need ten. These figures are merely illustrative. The actual calculations are extremely complex, and are necessarily secret. An informed guess, however, is that at no time between 1960 and 1963—the period of the so-called missile gap—will the Russians have a big enough lead to be entirely certain they could wipe out our retaliatory force. But our margin of safety is a narrow one.

"We can't, therefore, expect the old deterrent to keep the Russians out of Western Europe any longer—simply because the men in the Kremlin cannot believe (any more than we do) that it would be brought into action by anything less than a direct, unmistakable threat to the United States itself.". . .

During the last months of 1959 another set of facts sprang into view, inflaming still further the European doubts about the dependability of their American ally.

Throughout the NATO decade the United States had depended heavily on overseas bases. Even today the bulk of our nuclear striking force is made up of medium-range bombers, operating from fields in Europe and North Africa, and of intermediate-range ballistic missiles (Thors and Jupiters) based on seven sites in England, Italy, and Turkey. Because these bases were indispensable for our own safety, we had to be very patient indeed with the countries where they were located. That is one reason why we could never insist too hard that the Europeans make good their commitments to NATO, and why we poured such fantastic sums into the pockets of Spain's corrupt Fascist dictatorship. We had no choice.

But we soon will have. Toward the close of 1959, two technological developments indicated that we might not need those overseas bases much longer. (1) After many failures, our missileers finally worked the bugs out of the Atlas, an intercontinental weapon which now looks as if it will operate dependably from launchers on our own soil. (2) Enough progress was made on the Polaris weapons system to give some confidence that it may be ready for service within two years. By 1963, therefore, America's retaliatory striking power should be based partly on our home grounds, and partly on submarines capable of firing nuclear-tipped missiles while under water (and thus almost invulnerable to surprise attack).

When that day comes, many Europeans suspect that we may become reluctant to put up with the vexations and expense of an alliance which is no longer militarily essential to us.

These misgivings are reasonable enough. For the truth is that from a strictly military viewpoint NATO is becoming more of a liability than an asset to Europe and America alike. For the Europeans, it no longer provides sure, automatic defense, though it does threaten to embroil them in any quarrel that might arise between Russia and the United States. For America it offers little besides overseas bases, of rapidly diminishing value; while it costs us heavily in money and manpower, and keeps us constantly involved in dangerous arguments over such sore spots as Berlin.

Like a slowly accumulating poison, these unspoken doubts on both sides have been weakening NATO ever since the first Sputnik went into orbit. It would be impossible to pinpoint the date on which it died, but the first public admission of its death by a responsible European official came on November 23, 1959. On that day General Jean-Etienne Valluy, the NATO commander for Central Europe, chided the European members for not fulfilling their commitments, and for what he called their "moral disengagement."

"If this continues," he said, "General Norstad and I will be able to no longer hide the fact that we cannot fulfill our mission."

It *has* continued, at a faster pace. Indeed, General de Gaulle —the strongest and most realistic, if also the most difficult, of European statesmen—has been acting for some time as if NATO were already buried. He has pulled most of the French navy out of the NATO command, forced NATO bombers out of their French bases, and rebuffed all pleas to set up unified NATO controls, even for an air-raid warning system. At the same time de Gaulle has put France's resources under great strain in order to build, at the earliest possible moment, his own nuclear weapons.

This behavior has been dismissed, by some commentators, as a sort of *folie de grandeur;* but it may be nothing of the sort. It can be interpreted with equal logic as the behavior of a man who believes NATO would be useless in a pinch, and who therefore is determined to control his own forces and his own nuclear deterrent.

Another sign of *rigor mortis* is the growing popular revulsion in Europe against a strategy which relies solely on nuclear weapons. This reaction is often emotional rather than carefully-reasoned but that makes it all the harder to answer. How do you argue with a woman who feels in her marrow that a defense which means mutual suicide is worse than no defense at all?

A left-wing English Labour party politician recently put the case to me in these terms:

"In a crisis, one of two things can happen. Either you Americans will cave in, because you are afraid to touch off an atomic war; in that case the Russians win without a struggle. Or you will decide to fight; in that case, all of Western Europe will be destroyed, along with most of the United States.

"So maybe it would be wiser for the European countries—and perhaps even England as well—to pull out of the Alliance and turn neutralist. Then we would at least have a chance of avoiding destruction in a fight between Russia and America. Yes, I realize that no single country could hold off the Russians by itself. The neutralist course might well result in our being occupied by the Russians for a century—or two, or three.

"But dreadful as that might be, you have to admit, old boy, that it isn't quite as bad as extermination."

So far as I can judge, this view is not yet held by anything like a majority in any European country. But it may be held tacitly by many people who are reluctant to express such unheroic sentiments out loud—and it does seem to be spreading. . . .

Whatever their numbers, these people cannot be ignored, because it is hard to pretend that there is much vitality left in an Alliance which arouses almost hysterical opposition among even a sizable minority of the people it is supposed to protect.

Stated this way, the future of the Atlantic Community sounds about as bleak as a Dakota winter. But it may not be all that hopeless, since NATO might conceivably be replaced by a new kind of shield, better suited to the military situation into which the world seems to be moving.

To be workable, such a defense arrangement would have to meet five specifications:

(1) It must be credible. That is, everybody—friend and foe —would have to be convinced that it would actually be used against an aggressor.

(2) It must seem morally justifiable; its use must not jeopardize the future of the whole human race, as a nuclear war might well do.

(3) It must be clearly seen to be advantageous to all the nations taking part in it; the assets must outweigh the liabilities for all of them.

(4) It must be a plan they can afford to support—in terms of men and money—for an indefinite time.

(5) It must be capable of coping with any probable type of aggression.

Until a few months ago, it seemed impossible to devise any scheme which would measure up to all these requirements. Since the turn of the year, however, the chances appear to be improving—because of far-reaching changes taking place within both Russia and the West.

In Russia a slow evolution of policy has been under way ever since Stalin's death (or so it seems to many American specialists in Soviet affairs) and the shift apparently has speeded up since Khrushchev's visit to this country. As a consequence, it may be that the Kremlin has abandoned any intention of overrunning Western Europe by means of a massive invasion, of the sort which Stalin gave us good reason to fear. . . .

[It is believed that] Soviet leaders plan to move, not by direct military conquest, but by economic penetration, subversion, and diplomatic pressure. Apparently they really believe that they will win, eventually, in that "peaceful competition" with the West which they talk so much about—and with some reason, in view of the rapid growth of their economy. Military intervention might still be used on occasion, against a weak neighbor, but at least for the immediate future it seems likely to be a subordinate tool in the kit-bag of Soviet policy.

If this estimate proves accurate, what Western Europe will need is no longer a massive defense to beat off a massive invasion, but instead a new type of defense establishment designed to cope with the new Communist tactics. It would be essentially a constabulary—highly mobile and especially trained to handle subversion, local uprisings, border incidents, and the kind of probing attacks with which Communists habitually test the nerve and strength of their opponents.

Such a force could be armed only with conventional weapons, since nuclear weapons (even of the small tactical variety) would be unnecessary for its mission.

Recent changes within Western Europe—its astonishing economic recovery, the new-found stability of its governments, and the shrinking influence of local Communist parties—would seem to make this sort of defense force entirely practicable. If they make a serious try, the Europeans should have no great trouble in finding both the men and the money to keep it going indefinitely. [11]

A small American contingent—perhaps a division—might be assigned to the European constabulary as a token of our continuing sympathy and interest. But it should be fundamentally a European force, manned, financed, equipped, and led by the Europeans themselves. Nothing else would do so much to give our friends a sense of independence, self-respect, and responsibility for their own safety. And nothing less will eliminate the frictions and misunderstandings which are inevitable so long as the United States carries the main burden of patrolling the European frontier.

But the United States will still have to carry the main burden of counterbalancing the Soviet nuclear weapons. This entails a costly, constantly evolving system of Polaris submarines, antimissile warning networks, and intercontinental missiles in

[11] One of the most durable legends of the past decade is that the West could never hope to match the Communist hordes; and this supposed inferiority in manpower was a main justification for relying primarily on nuclear weapons.

As General Maxwell Taylor pointed out in his recent book, *The Uncertain Trumpet*, this myth simply is not true. The tabulation cited on page 138 of that book shows that Western Europe alone now has more than 54 million fit males of military age—while the Soviet Union has only 41 million. (If you add in 17 million men from the European satellites—of doubtful loyalty—the Soviet total would be 58 million.)

dispersed, "hardened," and eventually mobile sites. (For instance, the solid-fueled Minuteman, when it is ready three or four years from now, might be mounted on railway flat cars or river barges; shifting each missile a few miles every few days would make it infinitely harder for an enemy to zero-in on such targets, thus making a surprise attack far more risky.) The development of such a system should be our first military priority; for until the missile gap is closed, we can never feel entirely secure against a Soviet assault, improbable though it may seem at the moment.

Equally important, until we pull even with the Russians, they are never likely to agree to a disarmament plan with foolproof inspection. Only when we can sit down at the bargaining table with a hand as strong as theirs will we have much chance of getting a deal which we can accept.

Consequently the plan outlined so sketchily in the foregoing paragraphs would not promise any relaxation for anyone within the immediate future. On the contrary, it would demand greater efforts—a greater effort by the Europeans to build up a truly effective local defense of their own; a greater effort by America to regain our lost ground in the missile competition. (At the same time we should be strengthening our ground forces and providing them with an adequate airlift, to guard against brush-fire wars in the non-European sectors of the globe; but that is too complex a matter to touch on here.)

What it would promise—in the long run—is a realistic hope of disarmament; an awakening, eventually, from the atomic nightmare which haunts the world.

The main reason for such a hope is that an indefinite nuclear stalemate between us and the Russians just doesn't make sense for either side. Why should we both go to enormous expense and strain to keep up a stable of monstrous weapons which neither dares to use? If we can agree to scrap missiles and warheads—at the same time, and under conditions guaranteeing no deception—we would end up in exactly the same relative positions, militarily speaking. Both countries could then turn a vast treasure of material and brain power to more constructive uses. Even more welcome would be the removal of the constant fear that an atomic war might somehow get started by mistake. For so long as the missiles stand poised for instant take-off, there is always a danger that some colonel in Omsk (or Wyoming) might push the wrong button, or misread a blip on a radar screen.

Finally, both we and the Russians have an obvious interest in bringing such weapons under control before they spread to too many other nations. What kind of world will it be when every Nasser, Castro, and Trujillo has an atomic arsenal of his own? And with the latent rivalry between Russia and China on his mind, Mr. Khrushchev must spend an occasional sleepless night wondering what will happen when Mao Tse-tung can arm his fast-multiplying millions with such weapons.

For all these reasons thoughtful military men—including General Maxwell Taylor, one of the finest intellectuals our army has yet produced—believe that nuclear disarmament ought to be the No. 1 goal of American policy. Perhaps it is not too much to hope that somewhere in Moscow their counterparts are thinking along the same lines.

If and when that goal can be reached, we can then turn our full attention to what probably will prove the decisive struggle with the Russians: the struggle to see which nation can first build The Good Society, capable of winning the allegiance of the rest of the world.

IV. WORLD LAW AND
WORLD GOVERNMENT

EDITOR'S INTRODUCTION

The case for and against world federal government was presented twelve years ago in Volume 20, No. 5 of the Reference Shelf series (Julia E. Johnsen, *Federal World Government,* 1948). The passing of half an eventful generation has done nothing to add to or detract from the argument, which suggests that the World Government proposition is one for the ages and not for a day.

Still, there has been a subtle shift in the terms and tenor of the debate. During and for a few years after World War II, world federalists were vehement in their advocacy of immediate, full-scale action. That they are no longer so today reflects not their abandonment of this ideal (to them, a fundamental necessity), but their perhaps belated recognition that the world must first be made ready for federal government, and that progress, if any, will come in small stages—probably regionally rather than world-wide, by evolution rather than by radical innovation.

Supporters of the United Nations and world federalists, once friendly enemies, now work together in advancing the many aims of the only truly international organization possible under present circumstances, as well as those of agencies with more limited or specialized purposes.

Meanwhile, the talk is of "World Law," an idea by no means new especially to lawyers and scholars, but which was retrieved from near-oblivion by Vice President Nixon last year. Briefly stated, this position holds that nations will be tamed through the gradual accumulation of international legal precedents, to which they shall all freely and willingly subscribe. The sole institutional need is for a revitalized World Court, and perhaps some regional branches.

It is worth noting that advocates of World Law can be logically, though not necessarily, cool towards world federal government. As they see it, the success of the first makes the latter unnecessary. But this success rests on a major, and many will say questionable, premise: that all nations are basically of good will, that international conflicts are the fruit of misunderstanding, and that when shown the proper and legal way disputant nations will readily embark upon it.

The question here is, how much can World Law really accomplish, even given the best intentions of all nations which manifest their submission to it? More seriously yet, will all nations—and particularly those in the Communist bloc—adhere to this law faithfully? And what, finally, is the United States doing to promote World Law? These are the problems raised in the selections that follow Mr. Nixon's.

Whether World Law without an institutionalized power of coercion—a police authority able to apply sanctions and thus secure enforcement of adverse decisions—can long endure is the moot point. Optimists rest their case on the debatable premise already set forth; pessimists would bring the argument back to the classic World Government thesis.

That this thesis is still of very topical relevance is shown in the next selection, from *The Economist,* which clearly details how, willy-nilly, the world will have a supranational government if it will have disarmament with foolproof controls.

The section closes with an appeal by Salvador de Madariaga for all free nations to join in a world commonwealth as a rival and antidote to the universalistic designs of Soviet communism.

WHAT IS INTERNATIONAL (WORLD) LAW? [1]

"Too many people assume, generally without giving any serious thought to its character or its history, that international law is and always has been a sham. Others seem to think that

[1] From "What Is International Law?" reprint of British Broadcasting Company talk by R. Y. Jennings, Whewell Professor of International Law at Cambridge University, delivered as a review of *The Basis of Obligation in International Law and Other Papers,* by the late James L. Brierly, published by Oxford University Press, 1958. *Listener.* 63:51-2+. Ja. 14, '60. Reprinted by permission.

it is a force with an inherent strength of its own, and that if only we had the sense to set the lawyers to work to draft a comprehensive code for the nations we might live together in peace and all would be well with the world." This seems a fair summary by [James Leslie] Brierly of two widespread attitudes towards international law. . . .

What are the facts about international law? . . . International law . . . is a living, working system of legal principles, universally accepted, founded indeed in the actual practice of states and about as old as the modern state system itself. The Foreign Office of any developed country has a staff of lawyers whose sole, daily occupation is to advise upon innumerable questions of international law as they arise. . . .

What sort of questions are they which thus daily occupy the legal advisers of governments? Many of them will be questions about the interpretation and application of treaties; for the major part of modern international law is treaty law. To the layman the mention of treaties may bring to mind the precarious political arrangements we have read about in the history books and a recollection that the important treaty was once called "a scrap of paper." For with international law, as with all law, it is the breaches of it that command popular attention. . . . [But] even criminals observe the law far more often than they break it. And in truth, the many hundreds of treaties that the layman hardly hears about, and which are almost uniformly observed, are the very stuff of the normal, routine relations between states.

What do they deal with? . . . We find treaties dealing, amongst many other topics, with questions such as these: social security, copyright and patents, peaceful uses of atomic energy, international air services, weather stations, double taxation problems, fiscal evasions, contracts of insurance and reinsurance, death duties, fishery conservation, telecommunications, marketing and distribution of certain commodities, carriage of goods by rail and by road, and so on. These are not questions of high policy between governments; it is bread-and-butter stuff, directly affecting the kind of law that the man in the street may find himself come up against.   And in these questions, and hundreds like them into which international law nowadays enters, states do normally use the processes of law to settle their differences; they can and do assume as a matter of course that treaties agreed to will be kept and the generally accepted rules of international law obeyed.   Indeed, if these assumptions could not safely be made, the daily business of conducting foreign relations would in every country quickly grind to a standstill.

You may say: "This is all very well. . . . But what does international law have to say on the really big issues of high policy and power politics? And what happens if a big power chooses to defy it?"

"Reserved Domain" of the State's Discretion

Obviously, the layman is right in his suspicion that in this regard international law has not always been all that it might have been, to say the least.   But the trouble is not exactly where he supposes it to be; and it is important to get our facts right. For many people, I imagine, suppose that international law has always had plenty to say about these big issues but that nobody, alas, has ever taken much notice of it, except perhaps where it happened to suit his book.   But in fact the position is quite the reverse.   Traditional international law had only one thing to say about all these big issues, and that was that it had nothing to say about them because they all belonged to the "reserved domain," as it was called, of the sovereign state's own discretion.   In these matters traditional international law itself spoke the language of state sovereignty *verbatim*.

So questions like immigration, economic or financial policies, tariffs, armaments, forms of government, alliances, control of raw materials, treatment of nationals and national minorities— all these and much else belonged to this "reserved domain"— where international law entered not in except to confirm its own irrelevance.   This reserved domain included the right to war itself: for war was "no illegality," whatever its motive or purpose.   The law did not question but simply accepted the right of any state to wage war for any reason and to impose its will by force upon other states. The so-called laws of war were intended merely to keep the methods and instruments of war within some sort of bounds and to keep a nice balance between the commercial interests of belligerent and neutral. . . .

Such, then, was the position under what I have called the traditional law of nations; it was regularly observed by states but that was hardly surprising as it occupied a subordinate place in international relations; it was "a convenient means of settling disputes of minor importance or of facilitating the routine of international business." But . . . there have been great changes in the last few decades and especially since the close of the last war: changes which affect the whole nature and function of international law. To begin with, the content of the law has developed out of all recognition in scope, in degree of elaboration, and in sheer bulk. Indeed it has ceased to be merely a law between sovereign states. More and more it reaches down to . . . the "cross-frontier relationships" of organizations, of corporate bodies and of individuals. Whole new departments of the law have been developed, some with astonishing rapidity, to meet new needs: for example, the law, unheard of even twenty years ago, which concerns the exploitation of the rich under-sea resources of the continental shelf. Already equipped with a considerable body of case law, international law has become recognizably "lawyers' law," unlike the "mere literary instrument" as Sir Henry Maine called it, of seventy years ago.

Powerful Organizations

Moreover, the great breach in the system represented by the failure to provide a legal regime governing the use of force in international relations has been healed by the Charter of the United Nations which sets legal limits to the use of force by states. And, perhaps most important of all, in place of the completely decentralized international society of a generation ago, we find an astonishing proliferation of international organizations at state level of all kinds; many of them powerful, too, like the European Coal and Steel Community, Euratom, the International Civil Aviation Organization, the International Labor Office, the International Monetary Fund, and so on. Many of these deal with just such matters as even a short time ago were accepted as being well within the reserved domain of individual state competence. And finally, in the United Nations itself, with all its shortcomings, we have, for the first time in international relations, an international political organization which, with its eighty-two member states, is well-nigh universal: a fact of great political as well as legal significance.

This development of international organization in recent years tends to be stressed, for it was the lack of it that was the principal weakness of traditional international law. As Brierly said: "The real difference between international law and state law in respect of enforcement lies not in any principle but in organization." Later, he elaborated this thought: "Law is not a kind of cement with an inherent strength of its own." The strength of an internal system of law, he said, lay in the fact that it did not stand alone but was

> Just one element in a much wider system of general social organization; because, in a word, it is a part, but not the whole, of what we call government. I do not mean to suggest by this analogy that the progress of international law must wait for the establishment of an international government; that would indeed be a counsel of despair. But I do suggest that it cannot advance much beyond its present useful but modest role unless we can find internationally what I may call a substitute for government, by which I mean the creation of institutions which will enable the manifold functions of government, with whatever adaptations are necessary—and they will certainly be far-reaching—to be performed internationally.

But today we may safely say that this requirement is being fulfilled and that international law is indeed advancing along exactly these lines forecast by Brierly in 1944. This is not to say that the forces of legal isolationism and reaction are by any means spent. The idea of the "reserved domain" of sovereignty is still active in the form of a plea that a matter is one of "domestic jurisdiction": a dangerous catchword, for there is indeed little that is not within the domestic jurisdiction; but it does not at all follow that it is without international jurisdiction. . . .

Compulsory Jurisdiction

There is another way in which the development of international law is lagging badly; I mean the difficulty of achieving a reasonably large field of compulsory jurisdiction for the International Court of Justice at The Hague. It is not merely that compulsory jurisdiction is desirable for the disposing of disputes, though that is certainly true; but there is also the fact that a law which is only irregularly applied by courts tends to be an uncertain law. . . .

It is true, of course, that international law is increasingly applied by courts of all kinds, and not least by the internal courts of states; for matters of international law frequently arise in domestic courts, and when they do, international law is applied. The Hague Court itself has been kept busy one way and another, and has even in recent years decided some cases of the first importance, such as the Anglo-Norwegian Fisheries Case of 1951. Yet the fact remains that the court has relatively little compulsory jurisdiction; compulsory, that is to say, in the sense that one state may take another to the court whether the latter be willing to go or not. There is, of course, the so-called "optional clause" of the court's statute by which states may accept a measure of compulsory jurisdiction on a basis of reciprocity; but the coverage of such acceptances has in fact suffered a marked and persistent decline during precisely this recent period which has seen such great strides made both in the development of the substantive law and in international organization. It is true that there is at the moment reason to hope that the upward curve may have begun. The United Kingdom Government and the French Government have set an example by changing a far-reaching form of reservation which they both attached to their reservations only a short time ago; and there is strong hope that the United States Government may shortly follow their excellent example. But it will still remain true that the majority of states have not accepted compulsory jurisdiction in any form, with or without reservations.

So here again there is a popular fallacy. Many, if not most, people imagine that the weakness of international courts lies in

their lack of effective enforcement procedures. This is not so.
The true weakness is in many ways more serious. It lies in their
lack of compulsory jurisdiction. Of the several hundred awards
or adjudications by various tribunals handed down in the last
century or so, the number that have not been respected by the
losing party can be counted on the fingers of one hand with
something to spare. For that matter, it is important to remember
that the internal courts of states not infrequently have run into
heavy weather in dealing with really big issues. I suppose there
can be no court in the world with more real power than the
United States Supreme Court. But more than once that court
has been openly and directly defied. . . .

No: the real weakness of international tribunals lies not in
their lack of executive power but in their lack of jurisdiction.
It is important that this position be remedied, somehow or
other, because compulsory jurisdiction in the long run—maybe
even in the short run—is a necessary concomitant of the abolition of lawful forcible self-help. If the law forbids me to
assail my adversary, I do at any rate expect that it enables me
to hale him before a judge. A position in which force is forbidden but justice is voluntary is asking too much of human
nature.

This is not to suggest that all international disputes should
or could be settled by courts of justice. Even within a mature
system of domestic law, most people hope to manage to keep out
of the courts, and we recognize, too, that some disputes lie too
deep to be settled by court actions; indeed, we recognize even
within the state that some parties to disputes may be so powerful
or influential that the existing law has to be changed to suit their
contentions, rather than applied by a court. We must not, therefore, expect things to be very different in international society.
The judicial function has strict limitations of usefulness. Yet
it remains true that in a developed society it will always be
available at the suit of one party to a dispute; and this is certainly
no less true in the international sphere. It is a pity that so many
governments are still apparently so touchy about the possibility
of being made defendants before an international court. They

could learn much from the big corporations which regard litigation and even the losing of cases as matters of ordinary
routine. . . .

International law is neither a sham nor yet a panacea. . . .
Today, at any rate, international law is developing, perhaps as
never before. It certainly cannot alone bring about the kind of
international society we all would like to see; yet neither can
that society be brought about without the assistance of a developing international law. It is therefore an exciting subject
that lies at the core of some of the most urgent problems of
our time.

THE RULE OF LAW FOR NATIONS [2]

Men face essentially similar problems of disagreement and
resort to force in their personal and community lives as nations
now do in the divided world. And, historically, man has found
only one effective way to cope with this aspect of human nature—the rule of law.

More and more the leaders of the West have come to the
conclusion that the rule of law must somehow be established
to provide a way of settling disputes among nations as it does
among individuals. But the trouble has been that as yet we
have been unable to find practical methods of implementing this
idea. Is this one of these things that men can think about but
cannot get?

Let us see what a man who had one of the most brilliant
political and legal minds in the nation's history had to say in
this regard. Commenting on some of the problems of international organization the late Senator Robert Taft said:

I do not see how we can hope to secure permanent peace in the world
except by establishing law between nations and equal justice under
law. It may be a long hard course but I believe that the public opinion
of the world can be led along that course, so that the time will come
when that public opinion will support the decision of any reasonable
impartial tribunal based on justice. . . .

    [2] From address by Vice President Richard M. Nixon before the Academy
of Political Science, New York City, April 13, 1959. *Vital Speeches of the Day.*
25:421-4. My. 1, '59.

President Eisenhower . . . said in his State of the Union Message . . . [in] January [1959]:

It is my purpose to intensify efforts during the coming two years . . . to the end that the rule of law may replace the obsolete rule of force in the affairs of nations. Measures toward this end will be proposed later, including reexamination of our relation to the International Court of Justice.

I am now convinced, and in this I reflect the steadfast purpose of the President, and the wholehearted support of the Secretary of State and the Attorney General, that the time has now come to take the initiative in the direction of establishment of the rule of law in the world to replace the rule of force.

Under the Charter of the United Nations and the Statute of the International Court of Justice, institutions for the peaceful composing of differences among nations and for law-giving exist in the international community. Our primary problem today is not the creation of new international institutions, but the fuller and more fruitful use of the institutions we already possess.

The International Court of Justice is a case in point. Its relative lack of judicial business—in its twelve-year history an average of only two cases a year have come before the tribunal of fifteen outstanding international jurists—underlines the untried potentialities of this court. While it would be foolish to suppose that litigation before the court is the answer to all the world's problems, this method of settling disputes could profitably be employed in a wider range of cases than is presently done.

As the President indicated . . . it is time for the United States to reexamine its own position with regard to the court. Clearly all disputes regarding domestic matters must remain permanently within the jurisdiction of our own courts. Only matters which are essentially international in character should be referred to the International Court. But the United States reserved the right to determine unilaterally whether the subject matter of a particular dispute is within the domestic jurisdiction of the United States and is therefore excluded from the jurisdiction of the court.   As a result of this position on our part, other nations have adopted similar reservations. This is one of the major reasons for the lack of judicial business before the court . . .

There is one class of disputes between nations which, in the past, has been one of the primary causes of war.   These economic disputes assume major importance today at a time when the cold war may be shifting its major front from politics and ideology to the so-called "ruble war" for the trade and the development of new and neutral countries.

As far as international trade is concerned, an imposing structure of international agreements already exists. More complex and urgent than trade, as such, is the area of international investment. For in this area will be determined one of the most burning issues of our times—whether the economic development of new nations, so essential to their growth in political self-confidence and successful self-government, will be accomplished peacefully or violently, swiftly or wastefully, in freedom or in regimentation and terror.

We must begin by recognizing that the task of providing the necessary capital for investment in underdeveloped countries is a job too big for mere government money. Only private money, privately managed, can do it right in many sectors of needed development. And private investment requires a sound and reliable framework of laws in which to work.

Economic development, involving as it does so many lawyers and so many private investors, will tend to spread and promote more civilized legal systems wherever it goes. Already, in its effort to encourage United States private investment abroad, the United States Government has negotiated treaties of commerce with seventeen nations since 1946, tax conventions with twenty-one nations, and special investment guaranty agreements under the Mutual Security Act with forty nations. A host of other special arrangements are in effect, such as those under which we have helped six nations draft better domestic legislation relating to foreign investment. . . .

The great adventure of economic development through a world-wide expansion of private investment is bound to develop many new forms and channels of cooperation between governments and between individuals of different nations.

We need not fear this adventure; indeed we should welcome it. For if it sufficiently engages the imagination and public spirit of the legal profession and others who influence public opinion, it must be accompanied by the discovery or rediscovery, in countries old and new, of the legal principles and the respect for substantive law on which wealth and freedom alike are grounded.

There are encouraging signs at least that we are on the threshold of real progress toward creating more effective international law for the settlement of economic disputes between individuals and between nations.

Turning to the political area, we have now come far enough along in the great historic conflict between the free nations and the Communist bloc to know that negotiation and discussion alone will not necessarily resolve the fundamental issues between us. This has proved to be the case whether the negotiations took place through the very helpful processes of the United Nations, or at the conference table of foreign ministers, or even at what we now call the Summit.

What emerges, eventually, from these meetings at the conference table are agreements. We have made a great many agreements with the Soviet leaders from the time of Yalta and Potsdam. A major missing element in our agreements with the Soviet leaders has been any provision as to how disputes about the meaning of the agreements in connection with their implementation could be decided.

Looking back at the first Summit conference at Geneva [in 1955], for example, we find that it produced an agreement, signed by the Soviet leaders, which elevated the hopes of the entire world.

It should be noted however, that the President and the Secretary of State repeatedly warned both before and after the holding of the conference that success could be measured only in deeds. One of the announced purposes of the conference was to test the Soviet sincerity by the standard of performance.

The Summit conference has since been characterized by some as a failure, but in terms of agreements, as such, it was a success.

Let me quote briefly from that agreement:

The heads of government, recognizing their common responsibility for the settlement of the German question and the reunification of Germany, have agreed that the settlement of the German question and the reunification of Germany by means of free elections shall be carried out in conformity with the national interests of the German people and the interests of European security.

In other words, those who participated in the conference, including Mr. Khrushchev, agreed at Geneva on a sound method for dealing with the German problem—the very same problem from which he has now fathered the . . . crisis at Berlin. But while the agreement seemed clear, as events subsequently developed, Mr. Khrushchev's understanding of its meaning was ostensibly different from ours.

The crucial question remained—how was the agreement to be effective when the parties disagreed as to what it meant? This is typical of a problem that can arise wherever any agreement is entered into between nations. . . .

I do believe there is a significant step we can take toward finding an answer.

We should take the initiative in urging that in future agreements provisions be included to the effect: (1) that disputes which may arise as to the interpretation of the agreement should be submitted to the International Court of Justice at The Hague; and (2) that the nations signing the agreement should be bound by the decision of the court in such cases.

Such provisions will, of course, still leave us with many formidable questions involving our relationships with the Communist nations in those cases where they ignore an agreement completely apart from its interpretation. But I believe this would be a major step forward in developing a rule of law for the settlement of political disputes between nations and in the direction all free men hope to pursue. If there is no provision for settling disputes as to what an international agreement means and one nation is acting in bad faith, the agreement has relatively little significance. In the absence of such a provision an agreement can be flagrantly nullified by a nation acting in bad faith whenever it determines it is convenient to do so. . . .

The International Court of Justice is not a Western instrumentality. It is a duly constituted body under the United Nations Charter and has been recognized and established by the Soviet Union along with other signatories to the Charter.

There is no valid reason why the Soviets should not be willing to join with the nations of the free world in taking this step in the direction of submitting differences with regard to interpretation of agreements between nations to a duly established international court and thereby further the day when the rule of law will become a reality in the relations between nations.

And, on our part, as Secretary Dulles said in his speech before the New York State Bar Association . . . [in January 1959]: "Those nations which do have common standards should, by their conduct and example, advance the rule of law by submitting their disputes to the International Court of Justice, or to some other international tribunal upon which they agree."

We should be prepared to show the world by our example that the rule of law, even in the most trying circumstances, is the one system which all free men of good will must support.

MR. NIXON'S NOSTRUM [3]

Mr. Richard Nixon's speech before the Academy of Political Science showed that high degree of political unrealism that is the curse of the West, in its defense of itself against communism. The Vice President of the United States, whose insights into the

[3] From article in the feature entitled "The Week" in *National Review.* 2:6-7. Ap. 25, '59. Reprinted by permission.

munists among its constituents. And on the negative side, there would always be at least a minority of "judges" ruling solemnly in favor of the most recent Communist abuse of the law. It does no service to the law to increase the authority of any judicial body in which Communists are permitted to go about dressed as judges.

More than a waste of time, we regret to say. For Mr. Nixon tossed into the proposal a putative willingness by the United States to repeal the Connally Act of 1946 [see "The Connally Reservation" in this section, below] and be prepared, hereafter to surrender to the International Court the authority to decide whether or not complaints based on a treaty come under its jurisdiction. Conceivably a suit could arise in which some foreign government, appealing to some abstraction or other in the UN Treaty, or Covenant of Human Rights, might some day ask the International Court to set aside the United States immigration or education laws. To surrender in an age of *Machtpolitik* [power politics] the technicality by which we can, in the last analysis, assert our sovereignty over our own affairs is to stand guard over a shrine after ostentatiously tossing away one's rifle.

In a word: it does no service to the cause Mr. Nixon seeks to serve to go about solemnly advancing nice parliamentary devices for settling outstanding differences with the Soviet Union. To do so is to give life to the illusion that we are dealing with a law-abiding nation, concerned for the peaceful evolution of the affairs of the world. If anyone puts on a costume and participates in the sham, who will be left knowing that is what it is?

THE CONNALLY RESERVATION [4]

Those who believe the rule of law must be superior to the rule of force in the world . . . support repeal of the notorious 1946 Connally Amendment. This amendment hampers extension of the rule of law by a reservation that only the United States

[4] From "Time To Stand Up For World Law," an editorial from *Life* Magazine. 48:35. Mr. 7, '60. Copyright 1960 Time Inc. Reprinted by permission.

can decide whether the World Court may take jurisdiction in any case involving our nation. . . .

[There are] many people . . . even among lawyers, who should be the most vigorous advocates of the rule of law—who have been misled by the argument of unreconstructed isolationists (or pure demagogues) that repeal would undermine U.S. sovereignty. And some also fear that foreign judges may decide cases on ideological, political or nationalistic lines.

Actually, both these fears have little basis in reality, as any reasonable examination of the facts proves. The court's decisions have been generally excellent in legal reasoning, scholarship and judicial integrity—and furthermore those who take cases to the court usually obey its decisions. Among the fifteen judges, chosen by the UN's General Assembly and Security Council for nine-year terms, some have rendered decisions against their own nations. For example, a Peruvian, appointed as an *ad hoc* judge, decided against Peru in one case, and in another, won by the United States, a Soviet judge strongly defended the U.S. position.

As Arthur Larson's World Rule of Law Center at Duke University points out, the United States, with its billions invested in so many lands, needs the protection of law and the court's jurisdiction more than any other country. But so long as the Connally reservation exists, any other nation can use it against us, as Norway did against France (which had a similar reservation) to keep the court from ruling on Norway's repudiation of some gold bonds sold to French citizens. Last year even President de Gaulle, with all his touchiness about French sovereignty, saw his way clear to abolish France's reservation.

Some enthusiasts for extending the rule of law go so far as to claim that strengthening the World Court could establish world peace and order right away. That's too much to expect. But what it can and would do would be to build an accretion of precedents—of peaceful settlements of disputes accepted and obeyed by all the parties—which would help the world grow more orderly and less violent. As these precedents accumulate, smaller regional courts might well be established—for example in the Organization of American States—to judge such issues as the sort of expropriation which Cuba is now undertaking.

WOULD WORLD LAW AVERT WAR?[5]

Those who favor strengthening the World Court as an organ of the international community . . . believe that it is impossible to talk about international "morality" or invoke "the rule of law" against an aggressor as long as the world community remains at its present stage of development. Today, the world community is like a frontier town in the Wild West, with every nation claiming to be a law unto itself and carrying its own guns (or nuclear bombs) to defend its life, its honor, and its property. Such international law as exists is fragmentary and covers primarily such fields as business relations and maritime cases.

Thus the international community lacks the basic agencies of an organized society—a legislature to adopt laws, an independent judiciary with authority to decide when laws have been violated and a police force to carry out the court's decisions. Whenever it has been suggested in the past that such institutions should be developed, opponents have expressed fears that they would lead to world government and extinction of national sovereignty.

Assuming, however, that the World Court could be strengthened by the abandonment of existing national reservations to its jurisdiction and acceptance of its jurisdiction by the U.S.S.R., would this mean that the danger of war could be lessened? It is conceivable that the court could reduce many causes of tension between nations by interpretation of treaty provisions which produced conflicts. However, a basic problem would remain. Would the court be restricted to issues which are "justiciable"—that is, issues which are matters liable to a trial in a court of justice? Or could it pass judgment on "political" issues, which involve a vast variety of psychological, social, economic and other problems that create profound frustrations and hostilities among nations and call for settlement on other than legal grounds?

To take a problem which does not directly involve the East-West struggle, let us assume that France were ready to waive its jurisdiction over the Algerian war and permit its dispute with the Algerians, now regarded as a domestic matter, to be sub-

[5] From article by Vera Micheles Dean, historian, political scientist and author. *Foreign Policy Bulletin*, published by Foreign Policy Association-World Affairs Center. 38:135-6. My. 15, '59. Reprinted by permission.

mitted to the court. Would the problems at stake between France and Algeria, between the French settlers and the Moslem population, be susceptible of a settlement in court? Or do we urgently need a greater strengthening and refining of the political machinery of the international community if clashes of national interests are to be resolved under "world law" and on a basis of international "morality?" Even if the U.S.S.R. should vanish tomorrow, there would still be profound disagreements between non-Communist countries about international law issues . . . such as the use of force (at Suez) and recognition of governments (in the case of Peiping). The British political scientist, Harold Laski, used to say that the operation of a democratic society depends on a consensus of its people about basic issues, no matter how much they might differ about details. The achievement of such a consensus is today the fundamental task of the international society.

UP THE WORLD GOVERNMENT PATH [6]

In the month of March of the year of grace nineteen hundred and sixty, the governments of the United States, the United Kingdom, Canada, France and Italy jointly proclaimed their readiness to abdicate their sovereign authority, and invited all other principalities and powers to join with them in accepting the rule of a universal world authority that should bring lasting peace to a troubled earth. (Reader, read on. This is not one of *The Economist's* occasional fantasy pieces. Just the facts.) It was understood that their proposals were generally approved by the governments of Australia, Belgium, Denmark, Greece, Holland, New Zealand, Norway, Portugal, Turkey, and quite a few others. The full text of these somewhat historic propositions was duly published by various newspapers, and numerous commentaries were also printed. The net reaction of a public which is supposedly rather keen on lasting peace was resounding apathy.

Perhaps this is not so odd as it sounds. The five governments' shattering suggestion was made in the context of the

[6] From article in *The Economist.* 195:310-11. Ap. 23, '60. Reprinted by permission of *The Economist,* London.

long-drawn-out discussion about disarmament, which only a few persevering spirits have managed to follow through all its convolutions. And it was not, to put it mildly, spelled out very clearly for the lay reader's eye. But it nevertheless amounted to nothing short of a proposal for a world government.

In their joint disarmament plan of March 16, the five powers proposed the creation not only of a new international disarmament organization (IDO), whose task would be to watch over the process of general disarmament, but also (paragraph I.F.7) a separate "organization, to be an organ of, or linked to, the United Nations," charged with "preventing aggression and preserving world peace and security, as national armaments are reduced." This peace-keeping organization, which may as well be dubbed the PKO for short, would be initially established during the second phase of the five-power plan (paragraph II.J), and during the third and final phase its "build-up of international law enforcement capability to preserve world peace" would be completed.

It may be argued that this PKO would not constitute a world government, as its functions would be limited to those that the preservation of peace necessitates, and it would be given no powers to interfere in any other political field. Formally, that is correct. But form is not substance. In substantial fact, the PKO would inevitably find itself both involved in enforcing its own political decisions upon sovereign states, and (if the assumptions of the plan were realized) powerful enough to do so. Would that not make it a world government in all but name?

As regards its military power, there can be little room for dispute. If the PKO is to be equipped with enough military strength to enable it to prevent even the largest of national states from committing aggression, it must obviously be militarily stronger than any possible combination of nations. In the generally disarmed world under consideration, this . . . might require only a few quite small "conventional" establishments, distributed so that they could deal quickly with inflamed frontier disputes and so forth, and backed by a relatively modest—but unrivaled

—nuclear striking power. But it would have to be irresistible, or it would fall short of its stated purpose.

The proposition that the PKO would inevitably be drawn into political controversies is only a little more complex. One need not postulate the capture of the PKO by some guileful group of megalomaniacs intent on setting up a world dictatorship. It might be controlled, under the most elaborate system of safeguards, by the most dedicated and cautious team of Hammarskjöld-figures imaginable, and still find itself getting involved in matters that at first sight had nothing to do with its formal functions.

For the plain fact is that keeping world peace is not just a simple matter of occasionally calling upon an aggressor to refrain from trespassing across one of the frontiers that slice with such misleading simplicity across the map of our world. Let it first be remembered that a United Nations committee has spent several years trying to agree on a definition of "aggression," and has given up in despair. Let it be further noted that indirect aggression is today (not for the first time) fashionable. It is not done to issue a blunt declaration of war and send in the army (or the gunboats). It is more usual to set up a puppet rival government in some corner of the victim state's territory over which its legal government has failed to establish control, and then to respond to its appeal for aid; or to send in "volunteers" —properly organized, if need be, with tank divisions, lieutenant-generals, family allowances and periodical home leave . . . or to declare that one is intervening in order to prevent somebody else endangering the peace; or to say that the other fellow's maps are wrong and that the place your troops have seized actually lies within your own frontiers; or to give enthusiastic but formally discreet support to a guerrilla rising just across the line.

If the PKO were to let such complications deter it from taking any action, it would not be doing its job. If it were not deterred, it would be forced to take a political decision each time. If it relied on the United Nations to hand decisions down for it, it would find itself just as hampered as the UN has been by voting procedures and delaying tactics. If it were organized to take quick decisions for itself, they would have to be based on some set of principles. That in turn means that the PKO would have to think out a political program in advance of the crises that might come its way; and it would soon find itself assuming an openly governmental character.

Its foremost problem would be to decide whether it should automatically act to preserve the status quo through the world regardless of circumstances. If so . . . it would, for instance, be obliged to help Herr Ulbricht to suppress any German rising against his regime, for it would be impossible to prove that such a rising was not encouraged from West Germany, whose mere existence is an encouragement to sedition in the Democratic Republic . . . to force Tunisia to evict the Algerian rebel leaders and to stop providing their forces with lines of communication and supply . . . to guarantee the Trujillo regime in the Dominican Republic against any form of action that Cuba or other Caribbean countries might take to bring about the downfall of that petty dictatorship . . . to underwrite in perpetuity the existing bisection of Vietnam, Korea, Germany—and China. . . . It would have to stream like a thundercloud against the "wind of change."

The alternative, while less unthinkable, would be far more complicated. If the PKO took it upon itself to decide when and where the forces of change required the alteration of frontiers or regimes, it would be in the world government business with a vengeance. In Korea, for instance, it might find itself obliged to depose both governments and impose its own rule until the Koreans had established a sufficiently popular one to avert the threat of further conflict. Can one then visualize the same principle being applied to China?

It is hardly surprising that the five powers have been reticent about this aspect of their new proposals. What is more surprising is that the Russians as yet have not concentrated their attack upon it—or not, at any rate, at Geneva; the Soviet press was not slow to point out to its readers that the Western disarmament plan concealed an imperialist plot. Moscow must be aware that, in this age of nationalism, it could win support from many other

governments if it came out as the sworn foe of any notion of
world government—especially if this notion took the form of a
guarantee of the status quo. But it hesitates to make this move.
Can it be that, abhorrent though the whole thing seems to most
of the politicians for whom it implies dethronement from their
national dunghills, even the Russians suspect that among the
masses of the world's peoples there may be a growing readiness
to accept world government if that is the only real alternative
to war?

WORLD COMMONWEALTH [7]

It is obvious that the Great Schism is the chief obstacle on
the way to peace. We know . . . why. For . . . the core of peace
is freedom for men and nations, and the Communist party, in
control of Russia and China, is the sworn and outspoken enemy
of freedom.

How should the free world face the issue? "Talks" would
not appear to afford an adequate way, since they could hardly
lead to friendship with the rulers without leading to enmity
towards the ruled. . . .

The Soviet Union has a clear aim in view. It is far in
advance of anything the free world can evince as its own aim,
for two reasons: it has an aim while the free world has none;
and it seeks world unity, which is consonant with the need of
our day.

Why then is the Soviet Union rejected as a world leader by
every land and people both civilized and free? Because it seeks
to reach that aim by means inimical to human nature, since in
the process it abolishes freedom and public opinion wherever it
holds sway.

The first duty of the free world is therefore to rise to the
conception of world unity and world solidarity and to set out to
organize a world commonwealth. One does not leap to one's

[7] From "World Commonwealth: A New Look," by Salvador de Madariaga,
Spanish philosopher and diplomat. This essay was written in connection with
the fiftieth-anniversary program of the Carnegie Endowment for International
Peace, and will form a chapter in the book *Perspectives on Peace: 1910-1960* to
be published in autumn 1960 by Stevens and Sons in England and by Frederick
A. Praeger, Inc. in the United States. Reprinted by permission.

automatically in such an event. In view of the smallness of the French naval force and the form any war would be likely to take, this decision seemed on the surface unjustifiable and even meaningless. But it was the logical consequence of a chain of reasoning which has been adopted for the last few years by all observers of the new Soviet strategy. De Gaulle differs from others only in that he pushed this reasoning to its logical conclusion.

The starting-off point of this chain of reasoning is a fact that has been strikingly expressed by North Atlantic Treaty Organization Chairman Paul-Henri Spaak as follows:

The Atlantic Alliance was signed in April, 1949. In June the Russians ended the Berlin blockade. In October they ended the Greek civil war. They also stopped all their aggressive moves in Europe. But in the summer of 1950 North Korea attacked South Korea. At this time the Soviet threat entered a new phase, an African and Asiatic phase, which is still continuing and whose end no one can foresee.

It is perhaps true that the U.S.S.R. deems itself capable of putting pressure simultaneously on Asia, Africa, and Europe. But the development of the Berlin crisis from the end of 1958 to the beginning of 1960 showed that Moscow sees the Atlantic barrier as a sort of Maginot Line. Since it cannot cross this line without incurring the ultimate risk, it has tried outflanking maneuvers. And just as Hitler found an unfortified region north of the Maginot Line through which to ram his tanks (as the then Colonel de Gaulle had been warning for many years), so the Kremlin's strategists, looking at the part of the world not covered by the Atlantic Treaty, found the Western powers were carrying on a sort of cold war, not against Russia but against each other.

These Western dissensions resulted in the entry and consolidation of Soviet influence in a large part of the Middle East. They permitted the U.S.S.R. to play an easy and profitable game in East Africa, West Africa and North Africa. . . .

In his memorandum of September 1958 . . . [General de Gaulle] draws the appropriate conclusions from these facts: he asks that the Western Big Three—the United States, Great

goal at the first go; in political life, one must be content with
the possible. But, if one is wise, one must achieve the possible,
bearing in mind the desirable. Let us then define the desirable
and then outline the possible.

The Soviet Union seeks to unite the world by force. The
free world should seek to organize mankind by federation. The
United Nations is but an embryo of such a federation. It is
far too loosely conceived and far too demagogic, by which is
meant that, as an institution, it is not organic enough, indeed
not at all. It relies on the rudimentary method of counting votes,
which amounts to adding up pots and pans with horses and
books, ideas and operas. It is incoherent, unmanageable, and
unrealistic.

The ideal federation would in all probability be achieved by
grouping the nations first in federations naturally formed into
families by geographical, historical, and spiritual forces. The
following grouping is suggested as a concrete sketch, if only as
a basis for discussion:

There would be nine big units: the United States; the Commonwealth; Europe, up to the Russian frontier; the Soviet Union;
Yellow Asia; Brown Asia; Islam (from Pakistan to Morocco);
Africa, south of the Sahara; Iberian America. Each of these
groups would be governed by a council and an assembly. The
nine councils would appoint one representative each, and this
Council of Nine would rule world affairs.

We are not yet there. But the time has come to organize
the free world on a basis that would take account of this image
of the future. That part of Europe that is still free, the Iberian
Americans, the Islamic peoples, the Asians, should begin to set
up their several federations. Problems such as that of the French
minority in Algeria or that of Israel should be settled by special
measures under the international right of minorities; some countries might belong to two groups and act as links between them;
finally a number of permanent and temporary institutions should
be considered. Among the former a Free World Technical Aid
Center; among the latter a Free World Trade Commission to
monopolize all trade with Communist countries.

This, however, belongs to the realm of organization. It should be offered to the world as a model, rival to that of the universal Soviet Union offered by the Communist party. But the immediate need is to raise the true idea and ideal of liberty for all nations and for all men, instead of the false idea of peace, broadcast by the Soviet Union in order to stun and paralyze the free world. At every stage in our discussions, whether polemical or diplomatic, with the Soviets, we ought to insist on liberty. And, of course, in order to gain authority thereto we ought to see that liberty reigns everywhere in our free world.

V. CAN THE ARMS RACE BE CHECKED?

EDITOR'S INTRODUCTION

The world's most unfinished business is the arms race. No one has been more alive to this than the frontrunners in the race—Britain, France, the Soviet Union and the United States. During the last two years these nations have met in Geneva in renewed attempts to bring it to an end. It was hoped that the fifth major power, Red China, although excluded from the deliberations, would abide by the ultimate agreement.

As if condemned to the labors of Sisyphus, each side's negotiators saw one after another of their heavy stones, the so-called "substantial concessions," laboriously rolled up the hill, come rushing down again with a contemptuous shove from the opposition so that despite some real progress in procedural matters, agreement on the key issues of inspections and controls appeared as distant as ever.

Actually, Geneva was the scene of two concurrent negotiations—one for a ban on nuclear tests, the other for disarmament proper. The stumbling block in each was mutual distrust, the same force that inspires the arms race itself.

Then, on June 27, 1960, the Soviet delegation to the disarmament talks, followed by its East European satellites, suddenly marched out of the conference charging that the Western powers had shown no genuine desire to come to terms. The move came a few moments before the West was to unveil a new disarmament plan which it was hoped would overcome the objections that the Communists had raised against previous schemes. Although the Russians announced their intention to bring the disarmament question before the forthcoming United Nations General Assembly meeting, there was no prospect of an early resumption of serious off-stage talks.

The first article in this section, by Hugh Thomas, treats the question of disarmament from a general standpoint. This is followed by a comparison of the basic Western and Soviet plans.

Economist Seymour Harris then considers an important sidelight: the effect of disarmament on the U.S. economy.

The next excerpt is a brief account of the Russian withdrawal from the conference.

"The Nth Country Problem and Arms Control," a dire warning of the dangers inherent in the diffusion of nuclear weapons among an ever-increasing number of countries, serves as a preface to a *Time* article on the East-West test-ban strategy. This is followed by a summary of the accords reached in this particular negotiation.

In conclusion, Eugene Rabinowitch, a leading spokesman for American scientists, in an article written some months before the abrupt end of the conference, voices a thought held by many: that the Geneva negotiations were doomed to failure because they dealt with symptoms rather than causes. As a first step toward removing mutual distrust he recommends that we strive for world cooperation wherever it is feasible—as in the scientific collaboration of the International Geophysical Year.

DISARMAMENT: DREAM OR REALITY? [1]

There are four main reasons why disarmament . . . is often dismissed as being unworthy of attention. These are: (1) that a disarmament program . . . is technically impossible to achieve; (2) that even if technically possible, disarmament is psychologically impossible, since governments are not prepared to accept the necessary limitation of their freedom of action; (3) that armaments are the reflection of political mistrust and of other "international problems," and that therefore a disarmament treaty must await the settlement of these; (4) that even if technically and psychologically possible, the whole concept of disarmament is undesirable.

[1] From article by Hugh Thomas, former British Foreign Office official. *Political Quarterly.* 31:17-25. Ja. '60. Reprinted by permission.

There are flaws in each of these arguments. To take the fourth of them first: the benefits of disarmament would be partly economic, in that nations would thereafter be able to devote a greater proportion of their national wealth to productive purposes and that the international cost of essential raw materials would be reduced. The benefits would be partly military in that the possession of no, or fewer, arms would be less likely to tempt nations to consider the settlement of disputes by the use of force. A disarmament agreement would also have, as by-products, the moderation of the whole concept of irresponsible national sovereignty and the development of the power and prestige of the United Nations, under whose aegis the process would presumably develop. These would be considerable benefits. Very few persons would openly say that they would be outweighed by the obvious problems that disarmament would itself bring—such as the reemployment of those directly or indirectly engaged on the manufacture of armaments, or in the armed forces.

The realization of a comprehensive disarmament program would also pose certain political problems. Even if the treaty did not collaterally stipulate (as the Soviet Union have frequently urged that it should) the abolition of foreign bases, a reduction of the forces of the U.S.A. to, say, one million men would imply the wholesale reorganization of Western defense as it has been developed since 1949, and perhaps even the total withdrawal of American forces from Europe. Still, only a few people surely would say that the undoubted difficulties of this situation would not be counter-balanced by its other and real advantages. After all, Western defense, as embodied in NATO, was set up to meet the expansion of communism in East Europe under the shadow of the Red Army. If the Red Army were itself being cut to a minimum, it would be anachronistic to maintain Western military strength at a level demanded to meet the situation of ten years ago.

The second argument put forward in opposition to the whole concept of disarmament suggests simply that it is in fact too rational an approach to the problems of human organization. And, indeed, the idea that a group of men, some Soviet Communists, some Americans, sitting around the "green table" of international diplomacy, can arbitrarily sign away, into other channels, the present expenditure upon armaments takes a little getting used to. However, the mere fact that such a thing has not occurred before—at any rate on so comprehensive a scale— is not at all an argument against it being achieved now. Provided that the interests of the states concerned in an international project concur, there is no reason why the project in question should not succeed. Certain agreements have been reached with the Soviet Union by the Western Powers—such as those in Austria in 1955 and over the International Atomic Energy Agency. The military and economic advantages of disarmament after all exist for all states—though, of course, there may be some, in the Soviet Union or China, as in the West, who think these outweighed by the disadvantages. Before the Communist powers achieved a stockpile of nuclear weapons and before the Western nations achieved a relative parity in conventional weapons, these mutual advantages of disarmament were less apparent. Here the development of the world into two camps, with the uncommitted third also tending to act as a unit, and with the two camps already cooperating in the sphere of armaments, may assist agreement. Recent Soviet disarmament proposals are discussed below, but at this stage it may be said that their motives have been often impugned on very slender grounds. It would be wrong, that is, to argue that disarmament is *ipso facto* an impossibility because of the nature of the proposals hitherto made by the Soviet Union.

The third argument against disarmament has in it an element of truth in its formulation though not in its development. Of course, armaments, like war itself, express the suspicions between nations. "Political problems" are themselves the product of those same fears; and, if the understanding between two states is great, then even the greatest problems, which among other states might result in the development of the postures of hostility, can be settled amicably. In the same way, even the settlement of problems between two hostile states would not necessarily remove the general distrust between them. If, say, the problems of

Germany, Berlin, and Formosa were solved, there would un-doubtedly crop up other problems in, say, Syria or Iraq. Nor need an arms race, such as exists today, necessarily have anything to do with specific political problems. The nuclear arms race between America and Russia since 1945 has developed much as the arms race in battleships did between Germany and Britain in 1899-1914; both powers, on both occasions, have desired simply to get ahead—and remain ahead. The nuclear arms race, like the naval one, has been self-generating, and, in default of a dis-armament agreement, could be endless. In fact, a developing disarmament scheme could undoubtedly help to heal such inter-national disputes as exist, rather than need to wait upon them.

As for the first, physical, objections to disarmament, the question is chiefly one of inspection. For no one can question that it is perfectly possible for states to carry out all sorts of reductions of their military strength; what is important is that the world should be perfectly certain that they have done exactly what they have said they will do. For this reason, the actual measures of disarmament would have, to a great extent, to be dictated by the way that they can be most easily guaranteed. The detailed discussions, both before and since the second world war, about means of reducing conventional armaments and armed forces, suggest that a sure system of inspection would certainly be possible to achieve. The inspectorate would have to be large and with wide powers. It would have to have access to all military establishments, budgetary documents, and factories mak-ing and capable of making armaments. The various bodies which can be regarded as precedents for a disarmament inspectorate— the Inter-Allied Commission in Germany after the first world war, the non-intervention control system in Spain, the control bodies supervising the Indo-China and Korean armistices in 1955 —all gave perfectly accurate reports on what was going on. They may be regarded as partial failures, but this was because the governments to whom their reports were sent refused to act upon them. A small margin of error cannot be excluded, but, in the sphere of conventional armaments, this would be an acceptable risk. Technically, therefore, there is no reason why a conven-tional disarmament agreement should not occur.

The problem of nuclear weapons is quite different. No inspection system, with however wide powers, can guarantee that all nuclear weapons existing at the time of the signature of a disarmament treaty are eliminated, or converted for peaceful uses. The margin of error here might rise to 30 per cent. In respect of the future production of nuclear weapons the margin of error might be cut to 3 per cent. An approach to this problem might be made through inspection of their possible means of delivery—which, including missiles, are susceptible of more accurate guarantees. Nevertheless, even through this approach, it is impossible to hold out any hope whatever that, in the foreseeable future, any plan can be achieved which will give the world any certain guarantees that all nuclear weapons have been abolished. Nevertheless, there are several measures which *are* technically possible, and which, taken altogether, can be regarded as providing nuclear disarmament, while effectively limiting the likelihood of nuclear war. These would be: the end of the production of nuclear weapons—which, even if impossible to guarantee absolutely, would be acceptable *provided* that it was not accompanied by the total elimination of nuclear weapons; the delivery to the international atomic agency of increasingly large proportions of nuclear material at present used for war; a ban on nuclear weapon tests; a declaration that the means of delivery of nuclear weapons, including heavy bombers and missiles, should be abolished, together with the establishment, first, of some kind of observation system at airports and frontiers against surprise attack and, secondly, of a strong United Nations police force which might itself be equipped with such means of delivery as had been banned from the arsenals of separate states and which might be made automatically available to any state attacked by a violator of the treaty. But it would be along these lines at least that a disarmament system could be made to work. Thus, the final step of the total elimination of nuclear weapons would have to be indefinitely postponed. So long, indeed, as nuclear power remains in existence there will always remain the possibility that nuclear weapons can be made from material at present used for peace. In those states where nuclear weapons have once been made the technical know-how will remain and conversion from peaceful to military uses can occur in a few days. But one further safeguard might be found to exist in the very ease with which nuclear material can be converted for warlike ends. For this would force any state which proposed to cheat to think twice about any sudden threat to use nuclear weapons, since the threatened state might be able to gain such weapons between threat and action. An aggressor would have to prepare a very large-scale attack indeed if he was to be certain of eliminating all fear of reprisal. And it would be far less easy to prepare a big attack, without detection, than a mere sneak raid.

THE DISARMAMENT PLANS COMPARED [2]

These are the major differences between the Communist . . . [plan] and the Western:

The Communist plan calls for a swift timetable toward complete disarmament. In the first year to a year and a half, the armed forces of the powers would be reduced. In the next year and a half to two years, all conventional armed forces would be eliminated and foreign troops withdrawn from all bases. A final year would be set aside for the elimination of all nuclear, chemical, and biological weapons of mass destruction.

No timetable is provided in the Western plan. The first stage would consist of studies of every major disarmament problem and the first moves toward a reduction of armed forces and the establishment of depots for storage of conventional arms. The second stage would carry out agreements reached in the first, including cessation of nuclear weapons production, a ban on space vehicles carrying nuclear bombs and a reduction of military nuclear stockpiles. The final stage would eliminate nuclear weapons.

The difference in the timetable approach is fundamental. The Communists say the goal is all that really counts. The West calls for a balanced process that would not give the advantage to either side at any given point.

[2] From "The 2 Arms Plans: How They Differ," news story. New York *Times.* p 3. Mr. 17, '60. Reprinted by permission.

There is an important difference in emphasis as between conventional and nuclear weapons. The Communists would make no move toward nuclear disarmament until the third stage. The Western plan has conventional disarmament in all its stages. As for nuclear disarmament, the Western plan calls for studies in the first stage, actual steps toward reduction in the second and final elimination in the third.

The enforcement of disarmament also is an issue. The West envisages an international police force linked to the United Nations and strong enough to keep the peace. The Soviet plan has no such provision.

The current military positions of both sides also are reflected in a difference on the question of bases. The Soviet plan calls for elimination of all foreign bases in the second stage. To the West this represents an attempt to dissolve its Alliance before real disarmament takes place. Its plan makes no mention of foreign bases.

Under the Communist plan, nations would retain only forces needed for internal security. Under the Western plan, nations would be allowed to keep forces not only for internal security but to maintain their obligations under the United Nations Charter. Those obligations include military defense arrangements.

The Communists propose that the armed forces of the Soviet Union, the United States and Communist China be reduced in the first stage to 1.7 million men each and those of Britain and France to 650,000 each. The Western plan calls for the Soviet Union and the United States to reduce their forces to 2.5 million men each in the first stage and to 2.1 million in the second. The plan does not mention Britain, France and Communist China.

Both sides say the control organization must be set up before disarmament starts, that inspection must be carried out in every stage and that the duties and functions of the organization should increase as disarmament increases.

But it is precisely in this area that basic political differences emerge. The Russians say the Western plan is designed to establish a maximum amount of control without real disarmament.

The West says that on paper the Russians are willing to permit control and inspection but that their timetable and apparent unwillingness to examine every problem carefully in advance indicate that they do not mean it.

ECONOMIC CONSEQUENCES OF DISARMAMENT [3]

A cliché of Communist propaganda is that the "ruling circles" of the United States do not really want an end to the arms race because a large cutback in armaments would cause a depression.

The present defense budget of $46 billion—more than half of the total Federal budget and the equivalent of about 10 per cent of our gross national product—is obviously a factor of major importance in the economy. Can we prosper without it?

Yes, I believe we can. Prosperity is not basically dependent on defense contracts, but a sudden, sharp cut in defense spending would be a real, if temporary, shock to the economy. Effective government action would be needed to cushion such a shock; and, so far as I know, the government is not now prepared with an economic program to meet this kind of emergency. . . .

If we treat the years from 1941 to the present as a whole we find . . . that a period of record prosperity coincided with a period of heavy military outlays. . . . About one dollar out of seven went for war or preparation for war and this expenditure was undoubtedly a stimulus to the economy.

The question that faces us now becomes this: If we were to reduce drastically our outlays for defense, could we expect to repeat the heartening experience of 1946-1949 [when the national income rose, notwithstanding the sharp postwar drop in defense spending], or would we repeat what appears to be the more "normal" pattern of disarmament recession?

There are those who argue, on the basis of the post-World War II prosperity, that we can have prosperity with disarmament and without taking any special measures beyond a tax cut. The

[3] From "Can We Prosper Without Arms?" by Seymour E. Harris, Lucius N. Littauer Professor of Political Economy, Harvard University. New York *Times Magazine.* p 20+. N. 8, '59. Reprinted by permission.

Communist problem have often proved penetrating, . . . initiated a drive to give to the International Court of Justice, now the principal judicial organ of the United Nations, authority to adjudicate disputes arising between nations out of disagreements as to the meaning of existing treaties.

Mr. Nixon volunteered an unprofitable illustration. The difficulty between the Soviet Union and the United States, he said, exists not so much because there is an absence of formal agreements between the two nations, but because differences arise as to the *meaning* of the agreements. . . .

Mr. Nixon's solution: bring differences over the meaning of an agreement before the International Court for a settlement binding on both parties.

Mr. Nixon's proposal is a waste of time for the reason that it advances as relevant to the solution of our difficulties, judicial proceedings to which Communists are in principle indifferent. Any revolutionary worth his salt will eat Rule By Law for breakfast. The difficulty with Khrushchev over Berlin does not trace to his having misunderstood the meaning of the Geneva agreement but to his judging it no longer serviceable to the revolution, any more than he has found serviceable the forty-one treaties with us which, at last count, the Soviet Union has unabashedly broken.

The International Court of Justice is composed of fifteen men elected by the General Assembly and the Security Council of the UN, and so reflects the composition of the UN, which these days is split between Communist and non-Communist countries. The idea that one could approach such a court in any dispute in which the Soviet Union is involved and get other than a political decision, is absurd. And the suggestion that if the Court's decision were against the Communists the Soviet Union would submit to it is, once again, unrealistic. The implicit notion that there would be a residual advantage to the West in having the majority of the Supreme Court of the UN go on record as siding with us next time the Soviet Union tosses over a treaty, is, still again, naïve; for the UN has not, and will not accumulate moral force, so long as it numbers Commoney saved by taxpayers, they argue, will flow automatically into increased consumption and nondefense investment, while industrial research continues to develop new and improved products to keep the economy dynamic and employment high.

I do not believe it is as simple as that. For one thing, there were the special circumstances just after World War II that do not obtain today—the controls and shortages of the preceding years and the pent-up savings that created the postwar boom. Today, in contrast, we are in a period of high spending.

Moreover, our only large tax cut since 1952 on the whole favored those taxed at the highest rates, the well-to-do and the business firms. This kind of tax cut would heighten the probability that tax savings will be hoarded, or be used disproportionately for investment and inadequately for consumption goods.

A high rate of investment would increase the nation's productive capacity. This is all to the good, for it improves our capacity to fight the cold war. But our private economy is faced with the tough problem of selling what it can produce. This is the reason for Madison Avenue. We turn out more and more goods with a given supply of labor, capital and management. In one hour of work we produce more than five times as much as in 1880. One American farmer feeds more than twenty people; it was not so long ago that a farmer fed only five people.

Further, we do not have a "given" supply of labor; each year we add close to a million new workers. This, plus rising productivity, means that in each year of the next decade our output should increase by $15 or $20 billion over the year before. We must take this additional amount of goods off the market each year if we are to avoid unemployment. I estimate that each $8 billion of this increment which we fail to take off the market will mean one million unemployed.

Today government purchases for defense take $46 billion off the market yearly. Should this buying be curtailed, then the market demand for goods and services would have to rise by an amount roughly equal to the curtailment, in addition to the annual rise of $15 or $20 billion per year required to prevent unemployment. I do not believe that private spending will respond sufficiently or with enough speed to accomplish this.

Of course, our whole $46-billion-per-year defense program is not going to evaporate overnight. But suppose that it is to be halved—a reasonable goal for a genuine disarmament agreement. How can we accommodate a $23 billion reduction in the defense budget, plus the normal $15-20 billion increase in output, without severe dislocation and unemployment?

First, I suggest that about half of the defense saving, or roughly $11 billion, be returned to the public as a tax cut. . . .

Second, the remaining $12 billion, retained by the Treasury, should be spent directly on nondefense government programs.

I urge this government spending policy for three reasons. First, to cushion the shock of a defense cutback will require prompt action; provided it is planned for in advance, the switch-over to nondefense government spending can be accomplished quickly, or timed to coincide with the deadline in defense spending. Second, a rise in welfare outlays by the government is of primary benefit to the lower-income groups—and these certainly deserve to share in any benefits deriving from a thaw in the cold war and a reduction of the arms burden. Third, there is a clear national need for greater welfare outlays.

Under the pressure of cold war costs and budgetary stress the government has been underspending for years in such vital areas as education, urban renewal, housing, power, pollution, irrigation, conservation, flood control, navigation, forestation, airport improvement, highways, hospitals and health services, and social security. . . .

These and other social needs offer ideal substitutes for defense spending to help keep employment and output high. In part, the outlays would relieve state and local governments, now in serious financial condition because of rising demands for public services. Several years ago, the President estimated their construction needs at $200 billion in ten years; actual outlays were at less than half that rate.

As defense spending is reduced some cities and regions will feel the impact more keenly than others. Military outlays are heavily concentrated in industrial areas such as Michigan and the Great Lakes region and New England. . . . These states and regions would need special help.

Since, under my proposal, the Federal Government would continue to spend a substantial sum in place of part of its defense outlay, it can favor these areas above others. Another approach is the Area Development Program, which the Administration, as well as a number of senators, led by Senator Douglas, has sponsored. A substantial program would be needed to yield funds for planning and training of workers for new jobs and to contribute capital as a means of attracting new industry. Any improvement in the unemployment compensation program, such as was suggested in a bill introduced by Senator Kennedy last year, would also help the newly depressed areas to make an adjustment.

If the policies outlined here are adopted we may confidently expect that substantial cuts in military outlays will not prove disastrous to the economy. But these policies require planning now, to avoid delay when the time comes. We should prepare tax cuts, not wait to consider them only in response to falling income. And the government should now begin to prepare a broad program of increased nondefense spending, in anticipation of the day when swords may indeed be beaten into plowshares.

BREAK-OFF OF NEGOTIATIONS [4]

The official Soviet news agency Tass said last week:

The disgraceful act of sending a spy plane into the airspace of the U.S.S.R, the torpedoing of the summit meeting, Dwight Eisenhower's scandalous Far Eastern tour, followed by the breakup of the Geneva talks, are parts of one and the same aggressive policy, the purpose of which is to aggravate international tension.

The Tass broadcast was a commentary on a Soviet move that in itself had greatly heightened international tension. On Monday the Russians, followed by the Soviet-bloc satellites, walked out of the ten-nation disarmament talks at Geneva, thus dashing

[4] From "Arms Impasse." New York *Times News of the Week in Review.* p E 1. Jl. 3, '60. Reprinted by permission.

hopes for progress toward reducing the crushing burden of world armaments. The abrupt Soviet termination of the Geneva talks underscored the deterioration in East-West relations that had set in with the breakup of the Paris Summit conference last month. It also marked yet another tough move in the Russians' strategy of blowing hot and cold in their relations with the West. . . .

East and West have waged a world-wide cold war—and occasionally a hot war—over a number of explosive issues for the past fifteen years. There have been periods of negotiation, and the resolution of some minor questions. But the big issues —Berlin, Korea, the Chinese Communist drive for control of Taiwan and other Asian areas, the Soviet domination of Eastern Europe and its attempts to penetrate the Middle East and the neutral territories—have remained unsettled.

Throughout this period, efforts to negotiate a disarmament agreement have served as a kind of barometer of the cold war. The latest effort to negotiate a disarmament agreement began at Geneva last March 15. Five Western nations—the United States, Britain, France, Canada, and Italy—and five Communist powers —the Soviet Union, Rumania, Poland, Czechoslovakia and Bulgaria—convened as a subcommittee of the eighty-two-nation UN Disarmament Commission to work out the terms of mutual arms reduction.

After six weeks of negotiation, the conference recessed on April 29 in the hope that the Big Four at Paris would provide new directives to resolve the impasse that had developed at Geneva. The two sides were at odds over a Soviet plan for "general and complete" disarmament in four years with only vague specifications about controls; and a Western plan for step-by-step disarmament with each phase accompanied by rigid controls.

Paris, of course, provided no new directives for anything. But the Russians returned to Geneva with a new disarmament plan which called for elimination of the means of delivery of nuclear weapons as a first step—an approach advocated by the French—along with the liquidation of overseas bases.

The Western powers had serious misgivings about the new Soviet plan since it threatened to strip the West of its deterrent power before effective disarmament or controls were in effect. But the Allies urged the United States to consider revisions in the Western plan. They feared Moscow might score a propaganda triumph if the West stood pat in the face of the apparent Soviet concessions.

Last Monday, before the formal session convened at Geneva, U.S. delegate Frederick M. Eaton stepped over to the chair occupied by Soviet delegate Valerian A. Zorin. He advised him that he had returned from the United States with new proposals.

Mr. Zorin was unmoved by the Eaton disclosure. He stunned the delegates with the announcement that Premier Khrushchev had already sent messages to the five Western heads of government announcing that Russia was "interrupting" its participation in the ten-nation conference because the West, and particularly the United States, was not negotiating in good faith. Russia, Mr. Zorin said, would ask the UN General Assembly to take up the disarmament issue at its next regular session in September.

Each of the Communist delegates then rose to echo the Zorin charges. The Polish delegate, who was chairman for the day, then announced: "The work of the ten-nation committee is now discontinued. . . ."

French delegate Jules Moch was incensed. "This is a scandal! It is hooliganism!" he shouted. But the Communist representatives filed out of the chamber. . . .

Moscow's walkout at Geneva was generally seen as consistent with its rupture of the Paris Summit conference. The Russians probably realized they would achieve no major advantages in the Geneva talks. They may also have felt that they had exhausted Geneva's propaganda possibilities and that the initiative would now pass to the West with the presentation of new U.S. proposals. By largely blaming the United States for the breakup of the Geneva conference, as they had done in the case of Paris, the Russians doubtless hoped to undermine Allied confidence in American leadership and weaken the Western position. . . .

THE Nth COUNTRY PROBLEM AND
ARMS CONTROL [5]

Acute fears have beset us since the introduction of nuclear weapons of mass destruction. But we have occasionally found some comfort in the thought that peace might be assured by a "balance of terror"; that, while nuclear weapons are confined to just a few great nations with an enormous stake in the planet's land and people, an all-out nuclear war is unlikely. This balance is an uneasy one, involving many complicated factors and it impels a continuing race for new offensive and defensive armaments.

But the production of both atomic and hydrogen weapons by Great Britain, the more recent development by France of atomic weaponry . . . and the rumors of nuclear weapons research in Communist China raise disquieting doubts about the validity of the "balance of terror" formula. Atomic weapons may eventually become so widely diffused that there will be no equilibrium or symmetry in their distribution. Among their owners may someday be rulers—and perhaps even ex-rulers—who have no major stake in world stability. Indeed, it has even been suggested that eventually atomic weapons, like other powerful armaments, might find their way into the international open market, or that they might fall into the hands of outlaws and revolutionaries. . . .

This committee feels that the prospect of widely scattered nuclear weapons presents a very serious threat to world stability. This scattering was called the "third country problem" in the days before Britain had nuclear power; it was called the "fourth country problem" before France had the bomb . . . and it is now safer to call it the "Nth country problem." It is a challenge which is not receiving the very serious attention it deserves at home or abroad. It is also a possible opportunity—an opportunity to find at least one common concern which might move the nuclear powers of both the East and of the West to achieve some limited agreements for joint action.

[5] From statement by the National Planning Association Special Project Committee on Security Through Arms Control. (Planning Pamphlet no 108) The Association. Washington, D.C. Ja. '60. p vii-xii. © 1960, National Planning Association. Reprinted by permission.

Proliferation of nuclear weapons will inject incalculable factors into the equation of international politics. Some countries, under economic or other pressures, may eventually sell atomic weapons. Governments under fanatics or dictators may act rashly. The possibility of accidental or of unauthorized use of atomic weapons will increase. Irresponsible "mischief-making" by one small nation could catalyze a nuclear conflict between larger powers, or might cause pre-existing nonnuclear hostilities to escalate into nuclear hostilities.

The risk of accidental war by the mischievous action of a third party or by the possible mismanagement of tests, war exercises, strategic miscalculation, and the like is further enhanced by the rapid introduction of "quick reaction" systems. These tend to be inflexible, so that full-scale war may grow out of inadvertencies or deliberate mischief. It will become even more difficult to achieve and enforce arms control agreements, and much harder to inspire confidence in their effectiveness.

Since it is hardly reasonable to expect a nation developing nuclear weapons to refrain from testing them, world-wide radioactive contamination is likely to exceed predictions based on projected tests by the present nuclear powers only.

The Nth country problem derives urgency from the fact that we are approaching the point where it will no longer be possible for the present nuclear powers to control the spread of nuclear weapons. Once a nation has successfully completed an atomic weapons program, it will have nuclear stockpiles which can be stored without appreciable deterioration, which can survive changes of government, and which can be sold, exchanged, or given away.

The period, then, in which the major power blocs have a common opportunity to limit membership in the "atomic club" is, in the long view of history, a very brief one. We are now living in that period, and ten years of it have gone by.

The question of whether to invest or not to invest in nuclear armaments will be debated in many capitals during the years ahead. No aspirant can afford to ignore the grave difficulties and heavy expenses which confront a would-be atomic power, nor ignore the fact that a profuse capacity for destruction is not necessarily a source of security. It is certainly clear that atomic weapons projects are not, in the present state of the art, easy for a middle-sized nation to undertake. But standards of rational priorities of economic effort are not always observed, and from the days of the pyramids of Egypt, human needs have been sacrificed to concepts of glory. We cannot predict with assurance what nation will have, and what nation will not have, independent atomic capabilities in the years ahead.

A TEST-BAN PRIMER [6]

Who called the Geneva test-ban conference?

On August 22, 1958, President Eisenhower announced the suspension of U.S. nuclear tests as of October 31, 1958, and invited the U.S.S.R. to a test-ban conference in Geneva.

For what reason?

The Eisenhower Administration conceived a test-ban treaty as a possible step toward controlled general disarmament. In 1955-1957, when Russian propagandists were clamoring for a ban, President Eisenhower insisted that he would negotiate one only as a part of a larger package, including a halt in production of nuclear materials for weapons purposes, and other steps toward disarmament.

Why is the United States now discussing a ban apart from disarmament?

President Eisenhower and Secretary of State Herter hope that a test-ban treaty will be a "first step" toward disarmament. One of the biggest obstacles to any disarmament agreement with Russia is an almost paranoid Soviet wariness toward Western inspection and control proposals. Eisenhower and Herter think that if a test-ban control system could be negotiated with the Russians, it might be a "breakthrough" on disarmament control problems. . . .

What would the United States gain from a test-ban agreement?

[6] From article in *Time*. 75:26-7. Ap. 11, '60. Courtesy *Time;* copyright Time Inc. 1960.

The stopping of all above-ground tests by Russia and Britain (as well as the United States of course) and perhaps some progress toward making outer space off limits for nuclear shots. President Eisenhower and Secretary Herter also believe that it would be good to get the nuclear rules set up before other nations begin to manufacture nuclear weapons. . . .

Would the United States lose any of its present bombs by the treaty?

No.

How many bombs does the United States have?

The number is classified, but the United States does have a widely diversified and dependable "family" of bombs and warheads. These range from small, low-yield, light-weight weapons used by ground and naval forces to the big H-bombs carried by B-52's. Furthermore, there are nuclear devices for antisubmarine warfare, anti-aircraft, air-to-air missiles and intercontinental missiles.

Do the bombs and warheads deteriorate?

No, they need maintenance but they remain lethal.

Is the U.S. supply enough to obliterate Russia?

Many times over.

Would the treaty banning above-surface tests injure development of further big bombs?

It is generally conceded that the United States has all the big bombs it needs.

Would the stopping of U.S. underground tests hamper development and refinement of small nuclear devices?

The warheads designed for the Polaris and Minuteman solid-fuel missiles, which the United States is depending upon to close the missile gap in the mid-1960's, pack a nuclear punch of about half a megaton, compared with an estimated eight megatons carried by Soviet intercontinental ballistic missiles, and about three or four megatons in the nose cone of the U.S.'s Atlas ICBM. With additional nuclear tests, the yield of the Polaris and Minuteman warheads could be significantly increased, although Admiral William Raborn Jr. has said he needs no further tests of the present Polaris warhead. Some U.S. scientists and military men would like further testing to develop "clean" nuclear weapons with little fallout. The United States has developed small warheads, with a yield of less than one kiloton for use in tactical weapons, but so far these small warheads are "dirty," and the dirtiness makes it difficult for troops to follow behind the bombardment. (A kiloton is the equivalent in blast of 1,000 tons of TNT. The bomb that wrecked Hiroshima measured about 20 kilotons. In the strange vocabulary of nuclear weapons, a one-kiloton weapon is considered "small." A megaton is 1,000 kilotons, or the equivalent of 1 million tons of TNT.)

Would a halt in development of tactical nuclear weapons impair U.S. defense?

Some military experts think so, even if the U.S.S.R. did not evade the ban by carrying out clandestine tests. Development of tactical nuclear weapons making it possible for the United States to overcome Communist superiority in military manpower without resorting to mass-destruction H-bombs, has long been a hope and goal of U.S. military thinking. Former Atomic Energy Commissioner Thomas E. Murray agrees that the only way the United States can escape from the "balance of terror" is to shift from reliance on mass-destruction H-bombs to reliance on tactical nuclear weapons. A test ban, he says, would stop development of such tactical nuclear weapons. Many earnest men who might otherwise be willing to go along with a test ban are haunted by the possibility that the U.S.S.R. would find ways to evade the ban and develop nuclear weapons superior to the United States'. To guard against this possibility, the United States has insisted from the outset that any nuclear test-ban agreement must include an adequate system of detection and control.

How could clandestine tests be detected?

That depends on the kind of test. A test conducted on the surface of the earth or in the atmosphere is relatively easy to detect; it gives off radiation that can be detected at great distances and in minute quantities. But special difficulties arise with tests in outer space or underground. Testing in outer space is largely a theoretical possibility, but underground testing raises trouble-some detection problems here and now. Neither fallout nor radiation escapes, and the only way to detect the test is to use seismographic instruments to pick up the earth tremors. Since there is no sure way to tell from the tremor's "signature" on the seismogram whether it was caused by an earthquake or an underground explosion, inspection teams are needed to make on-the-spot checks of suspicious tremors.

Would a system of seismographs and inspectors be pretty reliable?

The United States thought so when it entered in the Geneva conference in October 1958, but learned in the Hardtack underground test series in Nevada in September 1958 that no detection system using known methods could be depended upon to detect explosions of less than 19 kilotons.

If Russia entered into a test-ban agreement, would she be able to carry out clandestine tests?

Yes. Underground tests of much less than 19 kilotons could be carried out with slight risk of detection. And by going to a lot of expense, the U.S.S.R. could carry out tests much bigger than 19 kilotons without much risk. Under the "big-hole" theory worked out by U.S. scientists, an explosion in a very large, spherical underground chamber would be muffled by a factor of as much as 300 to 1, so that a 100-kiloton explosion would set up no stronger a tremor than an unmuffled one-third kiloton explosion, and would thus go entirely undetected. Evacuating a big-enough hole half-a-mile underground would be exceedingly costly, but perhaps worthwhile if the U.S.S.R. very badly wanted to test a nuclear device bigger than 19 kilotons.

Is the Eisenhower Administration worried about the evasion possibilities opened up by the "big-hole" theory?

Worried, but not enough to pull out of the Geneva Conference. The Administration is going ahead, on the theory that no imaginable benefit the U.S.S.R. could gain from a nuclear test would be great enough to justify either a substantial risk of detection (which some think would entail a massive propaganda defeat for the U.S.S.R.) or the great expense of excavating a huge underground chamber (which would involve some risk because it would be difficult to hide the excavation work). More important, the Administration believes that the U.S.S.R. genuinely wants a test ban, partly because Soviet leaders are worried about a problem that also worries U.S. leaders: additional nations, notably Red China, may acquire nuclear weapons. In the Administration's view, Moscow's genuine interest in a test ban greatly reduces the risk that the U.S.S.R. might try to evade it.

TEST-BAN ACHIEVEMENT AT GENEVA [7]

There are three diplomats . . . [in Geneva] who sometimes seem to be acting like a crew of builders gone mad.

They build part of a foundation, quarrel about how deep and wide it should be, throw up a scaffolding, clamber up to build an attic, rush down to install a refrigerator in an empty kitchen, lovingly decorate a picture-window living room and then rush outside to look nervously at the foundations again.

The three are Geneva's nuclear negotiators—the American, James J. Wadsworth; the Briton, Sir Michael Wright, and the Russian Semyon K. Tsarapkin, assigned to the uncharted job of working out a treaty to ban tests of nuclear weapons. They are among the most able and painstaking members of their trade.

They work in that frantic way . . . because politics and science keep changing the plans or holding back tools.

Despite the strange working techniques, the fact is that in the safes of the three diplomats there is a collection of documents that adds up to a respectable amount of agreement on the mechanism of the treaty.

After almost a year and a half of negotiations and 188 meetings this is how the framework stands:

Purpose: There shall be a treaty whose purpose it will be to outlaw nuclear weapons tests and this treaty shall be effectively controlled.

Excluded from this treaty, in the Western blueprint, are small-scale underground tests. The Russians accepted this . . .

[7] From "Test Ban Parley a Slow Process," news story. New York *Times*. p 20. Mr. 20, '60. Reprinted by permission.

provided the West agreed to a moratorium on all tests during a specified period of research on detection methods.

Obligations: The parties to the treaty agree not to help or encourage any other country to carry out nuclear tests.

All parties agree to cooperate fully with the control organization, to provide transport to its personnel within their boundaries when officially necessary, to assign aircraft and weather or exploration vessels to routine checking duty, to provide aircraft for special air-sampling tests and to give inspectors access to suspected areas whenever the treaty authorizes inspections. They agree not to try to influence the employees of the organization, who will be international civil servants.

Punishment for violations: None, except the unwritten punishment of exposure before the world and the probability of the collapse of the treaty system.

Duration: The treaty shall remain in force indefinitely, but there is an escape clause that, in effect, is a sanction against violators and feet-draggers.

The treaty provides that any party has an inherent right to withdraw and be released of its obligations if the provisions of the treaty, including those calling for timely installation and effective operation of the control system, are not being fulfilled.

This means that if a country such as Communist China, whose cooperation might be essential to world control, refused to sign up, the West could pull out.

Organs created: There will be a conference of all parties to the treaty, to meet annually, or at the request of a majority, in Vienna, the system's headquarters. Each member will have one vote and no veto. The job of the conference will be primarily to advise and recommend to the Control Commission, but it will also approve the budget.

The key organ is the Control Commission, to consist of the three original members—the United States, Britain and the Soviet Union—and four others elected by the conference for two-year terms. The commission will appoint the administrator of the system and the three original signers' right of veto will apply in this case. The state of international trust being what it is, this means that the administrator most likely will be a neutral.

The commission will be set up to function continuously. It must meet on twenty-four hours' notice on the demand of any member, usually in Vienna. From the time of the signing of the treaty to the first meeting, the commission's work will be handled by a preparatory commission, consisting initially of the three major nuclear powers.

The commission's chief function will be to set up and supervise a detection and identification system. Voting shall be by simple majority rule, except in the appointment of the administrator and in budgetary matters (on this last the two-thirds rule will prevail).

The Russians will give up their demand of veto rights on the dispatch of inspection teams provided the West accepts their basic proposal of a small quota of inspection teams, to be arrived at through political negotiation.

The core of the control system is the detection and identification network, to be directed by the administrator. The United States has presented a detailed outline of this network in a special annex. This has not been discussed with the Soviet Union, but it is based on recommendations of a panel of experts that met in Geneva in the summer of 1958, and the Russians have accepted their findings.

The network will consist of 10 to 170 scientifically equipped control posts spread throughout the world. The posts probably will be distributed this way: twenty-four in North America, six in Europe, thirty-seven in Asia, sixteen in South America, sixteen in Africa, four in Australia, seven in Antarctica and sixty on islands.

There will be ten detection vessels, planes, laboratories and a headquarters operation in Vienna.

Still to be worked out in detail are the techniques for carrying out on-the-spot inspections and for identifying high-altitude tests through ground control posts or satellites. The United States does not believe that all high-altitude tests can be identified effectively.

It will take some years to set up a full control system. The probability is that it would have to be done in phases—perhaps first on the soil of the nuclear powers. This is still to be worked out.

The range of agreement provides the framework of the treaty house. There is still much interior decorating to be done.

There is disagreement on what countries aside from the nuclear powers shall be on the Control Commission. Each side wants to make sure it is never outvoted.

On the question of staffing, there is agreement that Russians on the one hand and Britons and Americans on the other shall provide two-thirds of the technical staffs at control posts in the three nuclear countries and in Vienna. But there is no agreement on the breakdown by nationality of the remaining third or on the whole composition of inspection teams.

Also unsettled is whether there are to be permanent inspection teams, as the United States has proposed.

Another disagreement is whether the research to be carried out under the direction of the Control Commission should include nuclear testing. "Yes," says the West; "No," say the Russians.

Explosions for peaceful purposes will be permitted, under rigid supervision. But the Russians do not at all like the United States proposal that nuclear detonating devices constructed before the signing of the treaty could be put aside in vaults and exploded later without international examination.

The major disagreements are not matters of framework or decorating but of foundation. Until they are settled there will be no treaty. These hurdles are:

Number of inspections: From the beginning, the Russians have insisted that only a small number of on-the-spot inspections could be permitted and that this number must be reached by political negotiation, without being based on technical factors.

As the West sees it, a full treaty would have to include a great and perhaps unworkable number of inspections. One estimate is that there would have to be at least 75 to 150 inspections on Soviet soil annually.

The United States says the number of inspections must be determined by figuring out the number of earth tremors that might not be identified positively as earthquakes and then inspecting about 20 per cent to see whether they are earthquakes or forbidden explosions.

If the work goes ahead on the basis of a limited treaty, the problem of full inspection will be set aside for the moment. The West says that to control a limited treaty the Russians would have to permit twenty inspections a year on their soil.

The Russians have never given a figure on inspections but say the number should be "Few." Just as important, they refuse to discuss the question of scientific calculations based on the number of probable earthquakes. They say the figures vary too widely.

High-altitude tests: The United States wants to include in the ban only those high-altitude areas where it believes current control methods would assure the spotting of violations. This would leave out a still-undetermined range of shots, probably beyond 175,000 miles above the earth.

If the work goes ahead on the basis of a limited ban, the negotiations will make an end run around a basic problem that has confronted them. This is that the great number of inspections needed to control a full ban was really unacceptable to both sides.

DISARMING DISTRUST [8]

Wars are fought with weapons. Since it seems that no nation can afford a war—modern weapons having made it too destructive—why not get rid of weapons? They have become terrifically expensive: so that, in order to hold its own in the arms race, a nation must spend a large part of its income, and occupy a large proportion of its population, with preparations for war. What could be more reasonable than to stop wasting funds and resources getting ready to fight a war nobody wants?

[8] From "First Things First," by Eugene Rabinowitch, noted physicist and editor of *Bulletin of the Atomic Scientists.* *Bulletin of the Atomic Scientists.* 15:361-5. N. '59. Reprinted by permission.

Disarmament seems to practically everybody the first order of international business. This is one point on which Khrushchev and Eisenhower, Adenauer, Macmillan, and Nehru sincerely agree. . . . Why then has no progress been achieved in disarmament negotiations, which have been going on for years?

In his recent speech to the UN, proposing total disarmament in four years, Mr. Khrushchev said that if disarmament were achieved the Soviet Union would be willing to pool its efforts with those of the West in directing the released funds and technological capacities to the advancement of the underdeveloped parts of the world. Similar thoughts have often been expressed in the West: If only we could reduce our weapons budget, how much money we could apply to constructive efforts in all parts of the world! This is obviously true—but unfortunately irrelevant to the situation; and often, it is largely a pretext for not doing more for constructive purposes in the world.

The arms race and the difficulty of effective control of any disarmament pact have the same—obvious and well-known—reason: it is the distrust between nations and societies. This distrust is in turn due to the justified apprehension, if not certainty, that the political aims of the various states and societies are diametrically opposite; in fact, that the main interest of one state or society is to weaken, if not to destroy, the other.

This kind of "national aim" has been traditional in all human history. Antique and modern states and empires have been built up by pursuing such aims, and have been destroyed when they failed in the power contest. . . . The conviction still survives in all parts of the world that power conflicts are the natural and permanent content of history. . . . As long as different nations pursue their national interest as their supreme aims and only occasionally pool their efforts in the pursuit of common interests (and this usually only when these common interests require opposing a third nation, as in the NATO pact), disarmament will not come. If a man knows, or reasonably believes, that his neighbor's purpose is to take away his property (if not his life), he will arm himself with the most effective weapons he can acquire. True, evident existence of effective police protection could persuade him to give up these weapons; but to hope for the establishment of an international police force, able to enforce proper behavior on nations as powerful as the Soviet Union or the United States, is to misunderstand altogether the state of affairs in the world. Police force can be established among individuals in a society, because the great majority of them have a common interest in preventing violence, and in protecting peaceful economic interests between them, and this majority is much stronger than the few individuals seeking to enrich themselves by violence. International police will not be possible as long as the society of nations is dominated by the very nations against whom the police force will have to be employed.

Community of interests is the key; disarmament and a world police force can come only after common interests have been widely recognized as exceeding in importance the divergent interests of the different nations. We trust those whose interests we know—or believe—are largely common with ours. Despite all the mutual accusations, particularly at election times, the Republicans trust the Democrats and the Democrats trust the Republicans, the Conservatives trust the Labourites and the Labourites trust the Conservatives, because they know that the areas of their common interest are more fundamental than the areas of their conflict. . . .

Common interests are established through cooperation. Or, perhaps it would be more correct to say that while common interests always exist, people become aware of them only by the experience of cooperation.

If nations postpone cooperation until after disarmament, disarmament will never become possible, however strongly and honestly everybody wants it. It has become a truism in the West, to which the East at least pays lip service, that disarmament is impossible without controls; but without mutual trust, controls cannot be effective. The East now suspects extensive controls as an espionage tool, and the West is obsessed with the danger of evasion from even the most extensive controls imaginable. Cessation of nuclear tests was originally considered the easiest thing to control; except for the extreme case of low-energy underground tests, all nuclear tests can be discovered by remote monitoring stations outside the country in which the test takes place. Yet, the possibility of this one kind of evasion has kept the international negotiations in Geneva frustrated for a year. In this case, the limits of uncertainty are so narrow, and the importance of possible evasions so questionable, than an agreement is likely to be reached in the end; but controls of really significant disarmament steps will be much more difficult, the acceptance of controls short of 100 per cent effectiveness much less likely, and the requirements of an evasion-proof control much more difficult.

The area of disarmament in which progress is least likely to be achieved, unless a very large degree of mutual trust is first established, is the abolition of arms which now assure each side in the world conflict the capability for a "second stroke"— retaliation if it should be first attacked. These are, above all, the strategic air force and rockets with nuclear warheads. Such weapons could be abolished only under the most reliable controls, impossible without extensive mutual trust. It is therefore futile to think of beginning disarmament with the abolition of "weapons of mass destruction," as the Soviet Union has long insisted. Significantly, Khrushchev's speech to the United Nations indicated recognition that proposals to begin disarmament with "abolishing nuclear weapons" are impractical. In this speech, for the first time, the elimination of nuclear weapons (and of their carriers) was relegated to a later—the third—in the proposed sequence of stages. The speech also contained a hint at the understanding of the present importance of foreign bases for the American retaliatory capacity, by postponing the relinquishing of these bases to the second stage of the disarmament program. . . .

There are areas of armaments, in which, at the present time, negotiations may be more promising. In the first place, this applies to all types of armaments which have lost or are losing their decisive importance. This means not only cavalry or battleships, but may mean in time manned combat aircraft, which is being put out of business by the development of missiles. . . . At some future time, the same may even apply to submarines, or other weapons of attrition in a long war—although the United States is not likely soon to renounce the possession of nuclear submarines, with indefinite cruising capacity and ability to launch intermediate range rockets with nuclear warheads, since such submarines are important deterrent weapons. . . .

The realistically estimated possibilities of disarmament are thus limited. They extend to weapons whose importance is either minor or decreasing, and whose abolition could be therefore accepted even with less than 100 per cent secure controls. They extend to nuclear weapons tests, because the need for continued tests is minor, controls are relatively easy, and small possibilities of evasion can be tolerated. In due time they may extend to weapons which are important only for "old-fashioned," prolonged war, such as manned planes, tanks, and submarines. The chances for disarmament are nonexistent—for the time being— as far as nuclear weapons and missiles are concerned, although these weapons—the most expensive and the most destructive man has ever devised—are primarily responsible for the present universal clamor for disarmament. Perhaps there is some hope for an agreement on the specific nature and deployment of these weapons which could provide assurance that they are not intended for a "first attack," but are adapted only to the task of a retaliatory strike—if this distinction is technically feasible.

I do not want to appear to be "against disarmament"; this would seem as wicked as being against happiness and prosperity. I believe that the search for mutually acceptable disarmament steps must be continued with all possible good will and open-mindedness, and that it deserves wide popular support. However, I also believe that to consider disarmament as the first and main item on the international agenda, and to expect great successes in this area, would be deceiving ourselves and the world. I believe that the first and main order of international business is to reduce the conflict of interests between the great powers, and to replace it by a growing partnership.

As long as the main interests of the two power camps are opposite, and the possibility of an open power conflict between them remains real, most if not all of the local territorial conflicts between them are insoluble, because . . . every solution is bound to involve a change in the relative power of the two competing sides. . . . The best that can be done at present is to agree to postpone these problems until the context of the world situation is changed—either through growth of a universal community of interests, or—probably earlier—through a change in the military aspects of the power conflict, which may reduce the importance of maintaining certain alliances, possessing certain advance bases, or having space for maneuvering outside one's home territory (as the Soviet Union now has through its domination of Eastern Europe).

We must watch for these changes, and not cling stubbornly to security concepts which may become obsolete—and this unfortunately may be more difficult for a democratic country, where learning and unlearning must be done by large numbers of people, than for a totalitarian system, where only the views of a small number of people—although particularly stubborn and opinionated people—must be changed. But, the most important thing we can and must do is to pursue, without hesitation and delay, stubbornly and imaginatively, the aim of enlarging the areas of common interest and cooperation. . . .

The four years' complete disarmament plan of Khrushchev may be pure propaganda; or, what is more likely, it may be something the Soviet leaders would really like to see happen (but about the chances of which they have no illusions). In any case, it is an ideal which appeals to people all over the world.

The United States should show the world an ideal not less exciting but more realistic than "complete disarmament in four years." We should offer the world a broad and imaginative plan for world cooperation, in all practically feasible areas. Science is one obvious field in which cooperation is possible—in fact, traditional. The International Geophysical Year showed how successful it can be, even between nations poles apart in their ideology and their political aims. Other projects of the same type are slowly getting under way—for example, international cooperation in the fight against certain diseases. It is deplorable that the American government is not in the lead in devising new plans of this type; that Soviet proposals for the pooling of efforts in the development of thermonuclear energy, and in space exploration, seem to find only grudging response in Washington. . . .

The tradition of international cooperation in pure science must now be extended to applied science and technology. In this field, too, America and the West should show an imaginative leadership. It is through this kind of practical cooperation that the peoples of different nations, and their political leaders, can gradually come to see in each other not enemies, not competitors, but partners in a common effort; and only through this feeling of partnership will they get rid of mutual apprehension. This seems a long and tortuous way to solve problems which now threaten our very existence, and it is difficult to give up the belief that these problems can be solved, much more rapidly and directly, simply by destroying the weapons, or beating swords into plowshares. But this slow and hard approach leads to the true source of the danger—the antagonistic and self-centered attitudes of the nations and societies—instead of being directed merely at its manifestations — the acquisition by nations and societies of all kinds of murderous implements. . . .

I [once] compared attempts to cure the world's sickness by disarmament, to attempts to cure a patient by reducing his fever, without attacking the causes of the latter. . . . Reducing the fever is often a useful thing to do. . . . But in the case of a man as well as in that of mankind, attacking symptoms has only a limited effect; and is often unsuccessful if the cause of these symptoms is a virulent infection, or a persistent systemic disorder. The systemic disorder that causes the fever of the arms race is long-established and violent; to attack its symptoms and not its cause will not bring mankind very far.

VI. UNDERDEVELOPED NATIONS: THE NORTH-SOUTH PROBLEM

EDITOR'S INTRODUCTION

"When our history is written I doubt whether the impact of atomic energy or the conquest of outer space or the great World Wars will rank even close to the awakening of the people of the underdeveloped countries as the most significant political development of this century." So says Paul G. Hoffman in the address which opens this section. In ever-increasing numbers thoughtful people are coming to agree with him.

There is no better index of this new awareness than the rising appropriations made by nations on both sides of the Iron Curtain for aid programs in Asia, Africa, and Latin America. In the West, both Britain and France have a long record of private and governmental investment in those areas formerly part of their sprawling empires as well as in their remaining overseas dependencies. The United States Government began modestly with its Point Four technical assistance program in 1948, now allocates about half of its annual $4 billion foreign aid budget to the "developing" nations around the globe. And other industrially advanced countries in the Western camp are under strong pressures to play an active role in this new peaceful offensive. In June 1960, for example, the German Federal Republic announced a $500 million easy-loan program for low-income countries. Other nations are expected to follow suit.

The plain, common, and urgent interest of the free nations in assisting the less developed ones has found acknowledgment in the plans for two new international organizations, both of which will probably start functioning in the very near future. One, the International Development Association, with an initial capitalization of $1 billion, will be closely associated with the World Bank and may become another UN specialized agency.

Its major purpose will be to furnish long-term, low-interest loans for needed development projects that are not, by ordinary standards, "good business propositions."

The other came off the drafting board in April 1960. Under the tentative name of Organization for Economic Cooperation and Development (OECD), it will eventually succeed the long-established Organization for European Economic Cooperation (OEEC). It will have a membership of eighteen European nations plus Canada and the United States.

The OECD was crystallized partly in response to appeals such as that of Sir Oliver Franks who, in a significant speech earlier this year, here excerpted, broadly charted its outlines. In a felicitous phrase, Sir Oliver sums up the new orientation as "the North-South problem," namely the question of the relationship of the industrialized nations of the north to the underdeveloped nations that lie to the south of them.

While both Hoffman and Sir Oliver stress that "in our relations with the developing people we do not make them feel that what we do with them and for them . . . is done only as a means of making sure that the Communists don't 'get at' them," still the unvarnished fact is that East and West are in deadly competition for the minds and loyalties of men thus far deeply committed to neither.

What this underdeveloped world means in communism's grand design is clearly spelled out in another excerpt from the expert study recently prepared for the Senate Foreign Relations Committee. C. L. Sulzberger, of the New York *Times,* then gives a chilling blow-by-blow account of how this grand design is translated into actual policies and individually tailored to countries around the globe.

His conclusion, that neither individual Western nations nor the free world as a whole has yet devised an effective counterplan, points the way to what may well become the most burning issue facing us in the immediate years ahead.

THE UNDERDEVELOPED WORLD [1]

The single most important event . . . [the] shrinking of the world has brought to this twentieth century is the revolt of two thirds of the world's people against continued acceptance of poverty, illiteracy, and chronic ill health. They believe that a better life is possible for them and their children and they are determined to achieve it. Out of their massive yearnings can come a better, more peaceful and more prosperous world or, if these yearnings are ignored, a world of growing tensions and explosive unrest. . . .

The dimensions and complexity of the problem are staggering. There are sixty member nations of the United Nations which, by any standards, would be classified as less developed, and some forty important less developed territories. More than a billion people live in these countries. Mainland China, which has its own sternly disciplined program for its "great leap forward," is not included in this tabulation. As to complexity, some of the countries have sound development programs, but most are uncertain what to do. Furthermore, the conditions in no two countries are precisely similar and unless the differences —of climate, resources and customs—are taken into account, aid programs are ineffective. . . .

When our history is written I doubt whether the impact of atomic energy or the conquest of outer space or the great World Wars will rank even close to the awakening of the people of the underdeveloped countries as the most significant political development of this century.

Helping the people in the less developed countries is not a new idea. For decades, church groups, private foundations and private individuals have supported educational, medical and religious projects. The colonial powers, some years ago, went beyond activities of this type and engaged in limited programs of economic development. But the concept that all the richer

[1] From "Interdependence—Fact and Opportunity," address by Paul G. Hoffman, managing director of the United Nations Special Fund, to the Chicago Rotary Club, December 15, 1959. The Author. United Nations Special Fund. New York. '59. Reprinted by permission.

countries, whether owning colonies or not, should in their own enlightened self-interest assist in the development of the less developed countries is new. It did not gain wide acceptance until recently. It found its first concrete expression in the founding of the World Bank [International Bank for Reconstruction and Development] in 1945, the International Monetary Fund, and somewhat later, in the Point Four program of the United States and the Expanded Program of Technical Assistance of the United Nations. It wasn't, of course, until the 1950's that these programs really got underway. In the same decade private foundations also expanded their programs, and several regional programs were initiated. . . .

Despite the wide range of developmental activities carried on in the fifties, the result in terms of improved living standards, that is in per capita income, has been very disappointing. Before giving you the figures, may I point out clearly that statistics as to population, as to income, as to gross national product in these less developed countries are not precise. They should be regarded as informed guesses. The informed guess as to the average income per person in 1950 in the one hundred less developed countries and territories is $110. In 1959 it should reach $125, perhaps as much as $130, a net gain of some $15 to $20 in annual income in ten years. This lack of progress is due in part, but only in part, to a rapid increase in population. There are 200 million more mouths to feed in 1959 than there were in 1950. It is also true that if outside assistance had not been increased in that decade there might well have been a decrease in per capita income.

The fact remains that an increase of even $20 in income per year in 1959 compared with 1950, or only $2 more per person each year, is not good enough. It is too slow, dangerously too slow, particularly when compared with increases in per capita income in the richer nations. The average increase in annual per capita income in the Western nations in 1959 over 1950 was more than $300—in the United States that increase was $550. Remember: in the underdeveloped countries the gain was $20. It is quite all right for the rich to get richer but disturbing and distressing to have the desperately poor people remain desperately poor.

The crucial decade of the 1960's is just around the corner. In that decade, if a really explosive situation is to be avoided, an acceleration in the rate of improvement must be achieved. Better living standards for these people is by no means a complete answer to all their problems but it would give them hope, and provide the indispensable basis of progress toward solving many of their problems. As an absolute minimum, the goal for the year 1969 should be an across-the-board average per capita income of $160 for people in the underdeveloped countries. This may seem very little to you; and it is very little. But remember that income per person in India is now less than $70 a year.

Can this goal be reached? Theoretically it should be easy of attainment. The underlying reason for underdevelopment is under-utilization of physical and human resources. There is a vast store of potential wealth in the soil, rivers, forests, mineral deposits and marine resources of the less developed countries. And there is an even greater potential in their human resources. But these potential resources will not be utilized to the extent they should be unless certain conditions are met.

1. First and foremost, a new approach is needed to the problem of the development of the less developed countries. The concept of the so-called "have" nations extending aid to the "have not" nations as an act of philanthropy must give way to a realization that all countries, whether their incomes are high, medium or low, must in their own self-interest accept proportionate responsibility for the achievement of a rapidly expanding world economy. Today no single country can achieve maximum economic growth except in a growing world economy.

There is a real danger to the high-income countries in this notion of the rich helping the poor. Actually it isn't charity but good business for the industrially advanced nations to assist in building the purchasing power of the billion people in the low-income countries. These countries, according to unofficial estimates made at the United Nations, will need in the next ten years something over $200 billion worth of goods from outside sources. This is something I will have more to say about later. These countries actually are the new great economic frontier.

From the standpoint of the low-income countries it is also important to get away from the concept of the rich helping the poor. As long as this concept holds there will be too many situations in which leaders of the low-income countries will feel that their problems can be solved by external aid alone. Nothing could, of course, be further from the truth. No low-income country can possibly make real progress toward self-sufficiency unless it has dedicated leaders eager to accept responsibility for development and unless its people are willing to make real sacrifices and put their backs into the job. Outside aid can help only those eager to help themselves.

2. There is also need for new thinking on the part of the donor nations as to the purposes of economic aid. It should have one purpose and one purpose only, to obtain the highest possible return in the economic development of the country to which it is supplied. The notion that economic aid can be used to "win friends and influence people" is fallacious and should be abandoned. Equally important is the annihilation of the idea that economic aid should be used as a weapon in the ideological war. As long as that idea persists, aid will be misdirected, needlessly costly and relatively unproductive. Let us recapture as a guide the wisdom embodied in the words uttered by the late General George C. Marshall when he spoke at Harvard University in June 1947:

> Our policy is directed not against any country or doctrine but against hunger, poverty, desperation, and chaos. Its purpose should be the revival of a working economy in the world so as to permit the emergence of political and social conditions in which free institutions can exist.

3. There must be a rapid speed-up in activities to prepare the way for the greater investment required to raise production and buying power in the less developed countries. By these pre-investment activities I mean technical assistance, and particularly the making of surveys of natural resources, the establishment of

industrial research laboratories and the creation of training institutes.

Each day at the United Nations brings new evidence of how little is known about the physical resources of the less developed countries—about their mineral resources, river flows and watersheds, and soil content, industrial potentialities, markets and the like.

Let me give you one or two examples. The Nile River is the oldest river known to civilization and yet it is only within the last year that a survey has been started in Sudan to determine how an important part of the waters of that river might be used in that country for irrigation and power. And one of the first projects of the [United Nations] Special Fund is a survey, now underway, to determine the needs and resources of Argentina for electrical energy. I could go on citing situations of unknown and therefore unused wealth for the next hour.

As for the human resources of the less-developed nations, they have been shamefully neglected. Only a very small percentage of the people who live in these countries have ever had an opportunity to acquire an education and only a few have ever had positions of responsibility. There is an immense need for training of all kinds, from on-the-job training of artisans to the more complex sciences of technological and management institutes. Skilled men are the very sinews of economic progress. Here, too, is an immense wealth begging to be tapped.

The needs of the developing nations for pre-investment activities are so great that the field should be open for any country, any organization, any group, to help in any way of its own choice. But in the United Nations and its thirteen specialized agencies reposes the richest experience that can be found anywhere in every field of developmental activities. The fullest possible use should be made of these facilities for the simple reason that by so doing much better results can be obtained at substantial savings.

There are three reasons why more use should be made of the United Nations. First, the UN has the whole world from which to recruit technicians. In its technical assistance teams there are experts from many nations. This assures an unprecedented level of activity in the cross-fertilization of ideas and in the application of modern science to age-old problems. Secondly, short-range political considerations do not have to be taken into account. The sound criteria so necessary if developmental projects are to be successful can be established and adhered to. Proof of the advantages that repose in a multinational organization is found in the record of the World Bank. Because it has been able to hold fast to sound criteria it has put out in loans some $4.5 billion without a default. And finally, assistance through the United Nations represents a truly cooperative effort, with no nation seeking a privileged position and no nation beholden to another. . . .

One of the reasons why I have put great emphasis upon the importance of pre-investment activities such as training and resources surveys is because of my belief that a sharp increase in such activities will provide a sound basis for the sharp increase in investment which must be made in the less developed countries in the 1960's if that modest goal of an annual income of $160 per capita is to be achieved. Increased investment is required to supply these countries with the foreign exchange they need to buy the products and goods which are available only in the more advanced countries. Let's get this clear: it isn't dollars or pounds or francs that are needed but goods, goods that the more advanced nations have to sell; goods which these underdeveloped countries would like to buy.

A careful estimate indicates that in the next decade approximately $200 billion worth of goods will be required by the less developed countries from outside sources. This figure refers to those countries' requirements of commodities of which they are not importers. These are mainly foodstuffs, chemicals, textiles, metals and a wide variety of manufactures such as clothing, footwear, cement, pottery, photographic supplies, glass, paper, wood, leather, rubber, building materials, tractors, machine tools. The $200 billion figure excludes what these countries export to each other or to the rest of the world in the same categories.

If their present level of exports continues these under-developed countries would have foreign exchange available to the extent of approximately $125 billion. This means that they will have to find sources for an additional $75 billion of foreign exchange. By diligent effort it seems certain that they could expand their exports during the ten-year period by not less than $20 billion, which leaves some $55 billion that must be made available through increased investment from the outside.

A part of that investment could take the form of agricultural products. In addition a substantial percentage could well be in private investment which is expanding rapidly. There also should be an increased volume of sound World Bank loans. My guess is that the total of foreign exchange which could be counted on through these kinds of investment is from $30 to $35 billion.

This leaves $15 or $20 billion which would have to be financed through what are popularly called "soft loans" but which, in my opinion, should really be called long-range investments. ["Soft loans" either cannot be serviced out of revenues resulting from the investment or are not credit-worthy at present time by normal banking standards, as when applied to construction of roads, schools, hospitals, etc.—Ed.] There are a number of institutions already in the field which are prepared to make investments of this type. One is the United States Development Loan Fund, another, the Commonwealth Fund and there are several others. And it looks as though a new multinational institution, the International Development Association, will be shortly added to this list. The $15 to $20 billion of investments which these institutions should make are risky. But certainly the advanced countries are justified in putting $15 to $20 billions at risk to help assure the future of the less developed countries. The United States alone is planning to spend $450 billion for defense in the next decade and nobody asks "Can we afford it?" Surely the industrial countries together can put into this economic development abroad the equivalent of one-twentieth of what the United States alone spends for defense. . . .

I believe that an investment in the development of the less developed countries is an investment in the future of the United

States. But that development won't take place unless you do your part in convincing the United States Government and, more particularly, the United States Congress, that assistance to these countries, provided it is administered soundly and on a business basis, is not charity but good business.

The stakes we are playing for are breathtaking. If, in the next decade, adequate financing is provided for pre-investment activities and the required investment funds are made available, ten—perhaps twenty—of the less developed countries will achieve self-propelling economies by 1970. By self-propelling economies I mean these countries will be on their own. Who can doubt the impact that such an accomplishment would have on the rest of the less developed nations which had not made the grade. In the 1970's many more would stage a breakthrough and before the year 2000, the poverty, illiteracy, and chronic ill health which have been the lot of most of the world's people since the beginning of time, would be a memory.

A NEW PERSPECTIVE FOR THE ATLANTIC WORLD [2]

It seems to me that the economic objectives to which we have been accustomed in Europe and the United States since the Second World War paralleled the attempt to answer the dominant political and strategic problem, that of East-West tension polarized in Washington and Moscow. The two aims we tried to realize were, first, the recovery of Western Europe and, secondly, the strengthening of world liquidity so that the international exchanges of trade would not break down through lack of the means of payment. . . .

While these two great aims . . . were common objectives of the peoples on both sides of the Atlantic and while cooperation between them was genuine and strong, nothing at all could have been achieved without the broad, imaginative, constructive initiatives of American policy. The Marshall Plan itself, the whole story of aid and assistance, the steady liberali-

[2] From "The New International Balance: Challenge to the Western World," address by Sir Oliver Franks, former British ambassador to the United States, at a meeting of the Committee for Economic Development, New York. Text from *Saturday Review*. 43:20-5. Ja. 16, '60. Reprinted by permission.

zation of the international trading policies of the United States during the period, are historical evidence of this truth.

But why do I dig back twelve years into the past? To remind you how greatly things have changed. In the late 1940's and through most of the 1950's we were quite clear about these international economic objectives in the Western world and worked steadily towards them: there was no problem of identification. But now Europe has recovered. The problems of world liquidity have been eased. . . . The contrast between now and the late 1940's is absolute. We have moved into a different sort of world.

This is why it is important to ask what are now our common objectives of economic policy on the two sides of the Atlantic. I suggest that today we have two, and they are related to a change in the broad political and strategic posture of our Western world. Earlier the problems of East-West tension were dominant: now we have a North-South problem of equal importance. It is connected with the former but has its own independent and equal being.

I mean the problems of the relationship of the industrialized nations of the North to the underdeveloped and developing countries that lie to the south of them, whether in Central or South America, in Africa or the Middle East, in South Asia or in the great island archipelagoes of the Pacific. If twelve years ago the balance of the world turned on the recovery of Western Europe, now it turns on a right relationship of the industrial North of the globe to the developing South.

There is a second consideration. If we in the Western world, in North America and in Europe, are to succeed in two dimensions, North-South as well as East-West, then it is essential that our economic strength be adequate to our tasks. This means a more consciously dynamic view of growth in our communities than we have perhaps had before. We have to grow fast enough to look after demands for improving standards of life at home, the requirements of defense, and the aid and assistance we must give if the world balance is not to be tipped decisively against us. We must have growth; but we must combine it with economic stability. Here is our second objective, linked to but different from the first.

Is it desirable or necessary to set up more international machinery to help realize these objectives? . . .

I believe that there are questions which need discussion in a forum which brings together the industrialized nations of the North if they are to be successful in finding means and measures commensurate with their aims. In saying this I am in no way undervaluing the work of existing institutions [i.e., the World Bank, the International Monetary Fund, the General Agreement on Tariffs and Trade (GATT), various organs of the United Nations, and the nascent International Development Association. Also, within Europe, the Organization for European Economic Cooperation (OEEC), the European Economic Community, and the European Free Trade Association—Ed.]. . .

What are these questions? Let me give a few examples. There is the question of how much the industrialized North can channel into the developing countries. There are questions of whether the necessary growth and economic stability in the industrialized countries can be sufficiently foreseen and provided for to make a given scale of constructive help possible. There are questions of the appropriate shares to be borne by the different nations of the industrialized Atlantic world. There may be questions of priority and order. There are certainly issues of coordination and programing. At present coordination between us is quite inadequate. There is no general program. There is instead a pronounced lack of continuity. . . .

Just as twelve years ago the balance of the world depended upon the fate of Western Europe, so in these coming years it will surely turn on the destiny of the newly developing countries.

We all know that many of them intend to develop at all costs. It is no use wondering whether it is wise. We developed ourselves earlier and they are now going to develop themselves in turn. They face a vicious circle. Low living standards and free, broadly democratic societies cannot produce sufficient savings for the rapid economic development they will not forgo.

They need more capital to increase output; low output prevents sufficient saving for capital.

This circle can be broken in one of two ways. It can be broken by tyranny which, by enforcing hardships on the people and holding down their standard of living, forces the savings for rapid development. Or it can be broken by capital from outside which gives a free society the chance both to develop and to remain free. This vicious circle for country after country will be broken one way or the other in coming years. . . . I do not understate when I say that the world balance will shift decisively against us if we fail to devise adequate means to realize the twin objectives I have identified.

This is basically why I feel sure that we ought to have a forum—as informal as you like—in which we can provide a basis for the political decisions which our governments should make in this new phase of world affairs. . . .

While it is true that the East-West problem remains, and that this North-South problem of the industrialized countries of the globe in relation to the underdeveloped countries is equal and related, it is important that in our relations with the developing people we do not make them feel that what we do with them and for them to enable their own free development is done only as a means of making sure that the Communists don't "get at" them. Surely they must not feel that they are only being regarded as means to this end.

You cannot subordinate North-South to East-West. It has its own equal and independent being. If we citizens of the United States or of Britain put ourselves in the position of the Brazilians, Indians, Egyptians, or whatever other people you like, they must surely feel that we are interested in them for their own sakes as members of the world community, that we believe in their freedom, their free development. Secondly, we must strive to make the free world larger and more prosperous, while keeping it free. This is our long-range self-interest, just as it is their immediate, direct, and national interest. . . .

We must not, so to speak, wear only one pair of spectacles. We have to wear two. And when we eventually wear the North-

South spectacles, we have got to look at the problem clearly, so that our friends in the developing countries feel that our interests in them are genuine, positive, and strong.

SOVIET EXPECTATIONS OF THE UNDERDEVELOPED AREAS [3]

One of the cardinal elements of the Soviet outlook is the belief that the revolutionary wave now sweeping across Asia, Africa, and Latin America is an important factor favorable to Soviet interests, perhaps decisively so. Although recognizing that this development is not of their making and may not be wholly subject to their control, the Soviet leaders advance at least three reasons for thinking that it works heavily in their favor.

First, and at the very least, they see a negative advantage in the disintegration of the world system of trade and investment between the Western industrial nations and their markets and the sources of raw materials among the underdeveloped countries. With nothing to lose and everything to gain, the Soviet Union can enjoy—and on occasion stimulate—the disintegrative effect of flaming nationalism in these areas. In the Soviet view, the rise of "anti-imperialist liberation movements in the exploited colonial and semicolonial nations" is one of the fundamental characteristics of this period of history, and the result can only be the decline of the Western powers.

Secondly, the coincidence of this development with spectacular Soviet economic and technological advances is expected to have the effect of increasing Soviet influence in these areas as a model of economic development. Moreover, as a result of this economic growth, the Soviet Union will be better able to influence these areas by means of trade and economic assistance.

[3] From *United States Foreign Policy: U.S.S.R. and Eastern Europe; a Study,* prepared at the request of the Senate Committee on Foreign Relations, by a Columbia-Harvard Research Group. United States. Senate. Committee on Foreign Relations. 86th Congress, 2d session. Supt. of Docs. Washington 25, D.C. '60. p 12-15.

Third, the Soviet Union feels that it is in a better position than are the Western powers to relate its interests to those of the nationalist movements. As an outsider, it is not encumbered in its relations with these areas by the necessity of balancing, as the colonial powers must do, the conflicting interests of an existing system. It does not have a strategic interest in stabilizing an unstable situation. It is not embarrassed by the dilemma of reconciling the colonial interests of its allies with the aspirations of the peoples of the underdeveloped areas though it may, as in the French-Algerian dispute, have to decide which way to throw its support. Most of all, because of its Marxist convictions, it believes that the "capitalist" powers cannot genuinely assist in the industrialization of the underdeveloped areas for fear of competition, whereas the Soviet system is free to give aid "with no strings attached." (This is the Soviet explanation of a situation in which it proceeds to build a steel mill in an underdeveloped area while U.S. technical assistance concerns itself with health, education, roads, ports, light industries and other prerequisites for orderly industrial development.)

Although these elements of Lenin's theory of "imperialism" have been among the most central and persistent ideas in Soviet ideology, and remain among the liveliest sources of Soviet confidence in the future, the situation has in some ways changed its character in recent years, and this has had its effect upon Soviet tactics and short-term objectives.

Classically, the Soviet leaders have visualized the transformation of underdeveloped areas as a two-stage process, in the first of which "bourgeois national liberation movements," with the assistance of the Communists, would achieve independence from the colonial powers, whereupon, in the second stage, the Communists would take over from the "bourgeois nationalists."

With many countries of the underdeveloped areas having become independent since the Second World War, the characteristic situation in Asia, Africa, and Latin America, with some exceptions, is no longer one in which the political thrust is focused on the simple issue of independence. The force of nationalism, although powerfully expressed in "anti-imperialist" sentiment, is directed into the more complex drive toward economic development and the effort of a leadership group to stabilize its power.

The problem facing Soviet foreign policy in these areas is not how best to achieve the transformation of these countries to "socialism" as soon as possible, but how to insure the most profitable immediate effects of this process upon the configuration of power distribution in the world. Therefore, in many of these countries, the interests of Soviet policy require the Soviet Union to strengthen ascendant elements of the "national bourgeoisie" —including such disparate groups as landowners, officers, journalists, teachers, lawyers—with military or economic aid. In Soviet ideology, this is still described as the period of the first stage of collaboration with "bourgeois nationalism," but it must be understood that general Soviet strategy, rather than the revolutionary transformation of these particular areas, is governing, in the present and immediate future period of Soviet policy. It should be understood, however, that the takeover stage is deferred but not abandoned. Preparations for the takeover continue meanwhile, as evidenced by the large-scale training of native cadres in the Soviet Union. The local Communist parties, which can function within the framework of legal political activity during the collaborative phase of Soviet policy, are prepared to shift to a guerrilla or revolutionary role when the second stage is judged to have arrived. On occasion there may be some difference of opinion as to whether the conditions are in fact ripe for the second stage, as was the case in Indonesia in 1948, when a Communist effort to break the alliance with the national liberation movement and take over power failed and was judged to have been premature.

An interesting aspect of this development in Soviet thinking grew out of the effort to find a strategic advantage in the neutralist movement. The classical Soviet position had been that there was no such thing as neutralism—people or nations were either in the 'imperialist" camp or in the camp of "socialism, peace and democracy." Even the newly independent nations, whom the

Soviet called "semicolonial," were thought to be pawns of the "imperialist" camp, so long as they had not moved over into the Soviet sphere. Since 1954, however, the Soviet leaders have come to perceive that the neutralist movement could be a strategic advantage to the Soviet Union. At the Twentieth Congress of the Communist party of the Soviet Union, Khrushchev recognized the existence of a neutralist belt of nations, which he called the "zone of peace," to be accepted as an ally against the "warmongering imperialists."

The essential point is that the short-run policy of the Soviet Union in the Middle East, as elsewhere in Asia and Africa, is a policy of denial. The central purpose for the moment is to achieve the denial of the geographical positions, raw materials and markets of these areas to the Western industrial nations. It is not, for the present, a question of expansionism in the sense of seeking to acquire these territories, nor of the revolutionary transformation of these countries into "Socialist" states. In the short-term perspective, the crippling effect upon the advanced industrial nations is a more decisive strategic factor than would be the acquisition of additional underdeveloped populations by the Soviet sphere. The Soviet leadership is not under pressure to obtain additional raw materials from the underdeveloped countries, nor does it seem likely that there would be a great advantage in the present acquisition of territories which would put a further strain upon Soviet industrial resources. But to be able to turn on and off the faucet on oil running from the Middle East to Europe—this, for the moment, would put into Soviet hands an instrument capable of important political consequences in a decisive industrial part of the world.

But this is only the first stage. As one observer has remarked after an interview with Khrushchev:

It was plain that in Khrushchev's view the "uncommitted" group of states was a sort of infant class or prep school through which the excolonial countries pass before graduating as Socialist states and joining the Socialist camp.

The next stage, belonging to a longer-term perspective, involves bringing to power in the underdeveloped countries indigenous forces oriented on the Soviet Union, and moving these countries toward membership in the Soviet sphere. Then, in that time and in that way, will be fulfilled Lenin's famous prophecy that—

the outcome of the struggle will be determined by the fact that Russia, India, and China, etc., constitute the overwhelming majority of the population of the globe.

RUSSIA'S COLD WAR BATTLE PLAN [4]

Almost exactly five years ago delegates from twenty-nine nations met at Bandung, in Indonesia, and formed the Afro-Asian bloc. The group is still far from coordinated and contains neutralist, pro-Communist and pro-democratic governments. Nevertheless it assumes an increasing international importance.

Indeed, the most vital "cold war" competition is the effort to influence the economies and capture the allegiance of under-developed Afro-Asian lands. Unfortunately, however, the West suffers in this contest from three disadvantages.

First of all, we are far less well organized as a disciplined political coalition to cooperate in joint endeavors; national rivalries remain. Secondly, some Western nations are themselves former imperial overlords; our over-all cause is therefore tarnished by past prejudices. Thirdly, we lack a blueprint for strategy.

Unfortunately, the Soviet bloc possesses just the advantages we lack. Of these perhaps the most important is a well-thought-out program covering all conceivable eventualities and designed to swing Africa and Asia into the Communist fold. This links economic diplomacy, propaganda, foreign policy and subversion in one over-all grand plan. A study of this strategy produces the following analysis:

1. In colonies, like Kenya, that have not yet gained self-government. Anti-Western prejudices are encouraged and the Soviet bloc identifies itself with nationalism. Communist party cadres are built up, and youth and labor leaders brought within

[4] Article by C. L. Sulzberger, New York *Times* foreign affairs columnist. New York *Times*. p 36. Ap. 13, '60. Reprinted by permission.

the Soviet orbit for indoctrination. Nationalist leaders, including exiles, are courted.

2. In states, like Guinea, that have just won independence. Moscow takes advantage of governing inexperience and ambitions for economic development. It grants swift recognition and offers aid, thus permitting installation of technical missions. Official visits are exchanged. Cultural programs mold the opinions of the local elite. Communists remain in the background and support nationalists while "democratic fronts" begin applying Left-wing pressures. Chosen agents infiltrate key positions. Antipathy to Western "imperialists" is fanned.

3. In relatively stable new lands, like the United Arab Republic. The emphasis is on promoting neutralism and quietly laying the basis for future Communist leadership of a "national revolution." Economically, efforts are made to undersell the West and to swell the number of . . . technicians [from Communist countries]. Priority is given to selling arms and gaining sympathy among the military.

4. In states, like Indonesia, approaching crisis. Efforts are made to split the ruling party into factions, stress economic dislocations and administrative shortcomings, and to develop agitation by street crowds, students and officers. Propaganda warns that Western "imperialists" plan to intervene. Front organizations disseminate antigovernment propaganda.

5. In lands, like Iraq, where the regime is overthrown. There is threat of civil war and a breakdown in government. Anti-Western prejudices are encouraged to run wild. Intimate ties are established between Moscow and the new bosses. Neighboring states are assured of Soviet benevolence. More experts are sent in. There are strong warnings against outside "intervention" and talk of troop maneuvers and possible recourse to foreign "volunteers." Mob violence, carefully directed, underscores these pressures and Moscow warns other capitals to keep their hands off.

6. In lands, like Burma, where attempts to upset the regime have been frustrated. Here, when local Communists are repressed and anti-Western attitudes toned down, the Kremlin

fights a holding action. Diplomatic relations are reaffirmed and links with local Communists disavowed. Officials are cautioned against Western conspiracies to force abandonment of neutrality. Communist leaders go underground or flee to prepare another round.

This is an exceedingly skillful and well-prepared approach. It reckons with any eventuality and is prepared to accept short-range humiliations for the sake of long-range goals. We could never elaborate a similarly cynical program, but if any democratic counterplan at all has been devised it is a secret. Neither individual Western nations nor the free world en masse has yet coordinated efforts to win the century's most significant political battle. This is a war, even if it is cold; yet we fight it without a strategy.

BIBLIOGRAPHY

An asterisk (*) preceding a reference indicates that the article or a part of it has been reprinted in this book.

I. EAST VERSUS WEST

BOOKS AND PAMPHLETS

Aly, Bower, ed. Free world security: the thirty-fourth discussion and debate manual. (National University Extension Association. Committee on Discussion and Debate Materials) Artcraft Press. Columbia, Mo. '60.

Butterfield, Herbert. International conflict in the twentieth century. Harper. New York. '60.

Goodman, E. R. Soviet design for a world state. Columbia University Press. New York. '60.

Heilbroner, R. L. Future as history: historic currents of our times and the direction in which they are taking America. Harper. New York. '60.

Hughes, E. J. America the vincible. Doubleday. Garden City, N.Y. '59.

Morgenthau, H. J. Politics among nations. Knopf. New York. '59.

Perla, Leo. Can we end the cold war? Macmillan. New York. '60.

Platig, E. R. United States and the Soviet challenge. (Foreign Relations Series) Science Research Associates. Chicago. '60.

Rockefeller Brothers Fund. Mid-century challenge to U.S. foreign policy. (America at Mid-century Series) Doubleday. Garden City, N.Y. '59.

Rostow, W. W. United States in the world arena. Harper. New York. '60.

Seton-Watson, H. Neither war nor peace: the struggle for power in the postwar world. Praeger. New York. '60.

Strausz-Hupé, Robert and others. Protracted conflict. Harper. New York. '59.

* United States. Senate. Committee on Foreign Relations. United States foreign policy: Basic aims of United States foreign policy; a study prepared by the Council on Foreign Relations. 86th Congress, 1st session. Supt. of Docs. Washington 25, D.C. '59.

United States. Senate. Committee on Foreign Relations. United States foreign policy: Ideology and foreign affairs; a study prepared by the Center for International Affairs, Harvard University. 86th Congress, 2d session. Supt. of Docs. Washington 25, D.C. '60.

United States. Senate. Committee on Foreign Relations. United States foreign policy: The operational aspects of United States foreign policy; a study prepared by the Maxwell Graduate School of Citizenship and Public Affairs, Syracuse University. 86th Congress, 1st session. Supt. of Docs. Washington 25, D.C. '59.

* United States. Senate. Committee on Foreign Relations. United States foreign policy: U.S.S.R. and Eastern Europe; a study prepared by a Columbia-Harvard Research Group. 86th Congress, 2d session. Supt. of Docs. Washington 25, D.C. '60.

Van Slyck, Philip and others. U.S. foreign policy goals: what experts propose. (Headline Series no 142) Foreign Policy Association-World Affairs Center. New York. '60.

Whitney, T. P. Has Russia changed? (Headline Series no. 141) Foreign Policy Association-World Affairs Center. New York. '60.

PERIODICALS

Annals of the American Academy of Political and Social Science. 324: 1-7. Jl. '59. Communist politics in the Western world. D. J. Dallin.

Annals of the American Academy of Political and Social Science. 324: 39-45. Jl. '59. Soviet-American antagonism: how will it end? Louis Fischer.

Commentary. 28:381-8. N. '59. Khrushchev's new cold war strategy. H. J. Morgenthau.

Current History. 37:193-243. O '59. American foreign policy and the Communist world [special issue].

Foreign Affairs. 38:171-90. Ja. '60. Peaceful coexistence, a Western view. G. F. Kennan.

* Foreign Policy Bulletin 39:145-7. Je. 15, '60. U.S. and U.S.S.R; the dangers ahead. H. E. Salisbury.

Harper's Magazine. 216:39-47. Mr. '58. How can the West recover? G. F. Kennan.

Life. 47:33-4+. Jl. 13, '59. My alarming interview with Khrushchev. Averell Harriman.

Nation. 190:464-5 My. 28, '60. Debacle in Paris. Alexander Werth.

Nation. 190:523-31. Je. 18, '60 Balance of blame. C. W. Mills.

New Republic. 140:19-20. My. 25, '59. Explaining Soviet intentions. Jack Raymond.

* New Republic. 140:9-11. Je. 22, '59. Has the Soviet challenge changed? L. J. Halle.

New York Times Magazine. p 14+. N. 15, '59. Struggle called coexistence. L. J. Halle.

Progressive. 22:47-9. Mr. '58. Changing Soviet tactics in foreign affairs, M. Gordey.

Reader's Digest. 74:199-202. Je. '59. As the Kremlin sees a conference; excerpt from What we must know about communism. Henry and Bonaro Overstreet.

Saturday Evening Post. 232:32-3+. Ag. 15, '59. World in revolution. Robert Strausz-Hupé.

U.S. News & World Report. 48:37-9. F. 22, '60. Is the cold war now to heat up?

U.S. News & World Report. 48:124+. Mr. 14, '60. Khrushchev's summit plot. D. G. Acheson.

U.S. News & World Report. 48:43-5. My. 23, '60. Is Russia really changing her spots?

U.S. News & World Report. 48:41-4. Je. 6, '60. Where the war stands now: the Khrushchev mystery.

Vital Speeches of the Day. 26:39-41. N. 1, '59. Soviet world strategy. D. L. Miller.

II. THE UNITED NATIONS

BOOKS AND PAMPHLETS

Clark, Grenville and Sohn, L B. World peace through world law. 2d ed. Harvard University Press. Cambridge, Mass. '60.

Commission to Study the Organization of Peace. Organizing peace in the nuclear age. New York University Press. New York. '59.

Commission to Study the Organization of Peace. Strengthening the United Nations. Harper. New York. '57.

Courlander, Harold. Shaping our time: what the UN is and does. Oceana. New York. '60.

Coyle, D. C. United Nations and how it works. (Mentor Books) New American Library. New York. '58.

Eichelberger, Clark. United Nations: the first fifteen years. Harper. New York. '60.

Everyman's United Nations. 6th ed. International Documents Service, Columbia University Press. New York. '59.

Frey, W. R. United Nations peace force. Oceana. New York. '57.

Goodrich, L. M. United Nations. Crowell. New York. '59.

Goodrich, L. M. and Simons, A. P. United Nations and maintenance of peace and security. Brookings Institution. Washington, D.C. '55.

Hovet, Thomas, Jr. Bloc politics in the U.N. Harvard University Press. Cambridge, Mass. '60.

* Jessup, P. C. What the United States should do; press-release extracts from address at annual meeting of Conference Group of U.S. National Organizations on the United Nations, New York City May 4, 1960. Carnegie Endowment for International Peace. New York. '60.

Logue, J. J. Great debate on charter reform; a proposal for a stronger United Nations. Fordham University Press. New York. '58.

MacIver, R. M. Nations and the United Nations. Carnegie Endowment for International Peace. New York. '59.

Munro, Sir Leslie. United Nations: hope for a divided world. Holt. New York. '60.

Nicholas, H. G. United Nations as a political institution. Oxford University Press. New York. '59.

Riggs, R. E. Politics in the United Nations. University of Illinois Press. Urbana. '58.

Wilcox, F. O. and Marcy, C. M. Proposals for changes in the United Nations. Brookings Institution. Washington, D.C. '55.

PERIODICALS

Christian Century. 76:1043. S. 16, '59. United Nations' role in diplomacy.

*Commentary. 26:375-82. N. '58. New United Nations: what it can't and can do. H. J. Morgenthau.

*Commonweal. 69:615-17. Mr. 13, '59. U.N. police force? R. C. Good.

Current History. 37:228-32+. O. '59. United Nations and the cold war conflict. R. N. Berkes.

Current History. 38:321-57. Je. '60. United Nations and free world security [special issue].

*Economist. 194:12-13. Ja. 2, '60. Mr. Hammarskjöld, we presume.

Foreign Affairs. 36:597-610. Jl. '58. U.N. and national security. L. P. Bloomfield.

Foreign Affairs. 38:209-18. Ja. '60. Can the U.N. enforce peace? Sir Leslie Munro.

*Foreign Policy Bulletin. 36:85-7. F. 15, '57. How can the UN be strengthened? Quincy Wright.

*New Leader. 41:12-16. Ja. 27, '58. N.A.T.O. and the U.N. E. A. Gross.

New York Times Magazine. p 8+. Jl. 27, '58. Case for a standing U.N. army. Sir Leslie Munro.

*New York Times Magazine. p 12+. S. 21, '58. U.N. record and U.N. dilemma. E. A. Gross.

*New York Times Magazine p 14+. S. 27, '59. What future for the United Nations? L. B. Pearson.

Reporter. 16:30-2. Mr. 7, '57. U.N. is not a world government. Reinhold Niebuhr.

Saturday Evening Post. 230:25+. F. 15, '58. Is the U.N. old and tired? Demaree Bess.

Saturday Review. 43:22-3. Je. 4, '60. Permanent Summit. C. P. Romulo.

*Swiss Review of World Affairs. 10:20-2. F. '60. Changing United Nations. Max Beer.

United Nations Review. 4:6-10. My. '58. Vital role of the United Nations in a diplomacy of reconciliation. Dag Hammarskjöld.

United Nations Review. 6:26-32. Je. '60. Development of a constitutional framework for international cooperation. Dag Hammarskjöld.

Vital Speeches of the Day. 23:295-9. Mr. 1, '57. United Nations organization, in its present form it cannot work. Lord Cherwell.

Western World. 2:43-7. F. '59. Allies, NATO and the United Nations. E. H. Kloman.

Yale Review. 46:551-65. Je. '57. Metamorphosis of the United Nations. V. V. Aspaturian.

III. NATO AT THE CROSSROADS

BOOKS AND PAMPHLETS

Ball, M. M. NATO and the European Union movement. Praeger. New York. '59.

*Buchan, Alastair. NATO in the 1960's. Praeger. New York. '60.

Deutsch, K. W. and others. Political community and the North Atlantic area. Princeton University Press. Princeton, N.J. '57.

Knorr, Klaus, ed. NATO and American security. Princeton University Press. Princeton, N.J. '59.

Kraus, Michael. North Atlantic civilization. (Anvil Books) Van Nostrand. Princeton, N.J. '57.

Moore, B. T. NATO and the future of Europe. Harper. New York. '58.

Salvadori, Massimo. NATO: a twentieth century community of nations. (Anvil Books) Van Nostrand. Princeton, N.J. '57.

Taylor, M. D. Uncertain trumpet. Harper. New York. '60.

United States. Department of State. NATO, 1949-1959: the first ten years. (Publication 6783) Supt. of Docs. Washington 25, D.C. '59.

PERIODICALS

Annals of the American Academy of Political and Social Science. 312: 77-83. Jl. '57. Sources of tension between Western Europe and the United States. H. J. Morgenthau.

Annals of the American Academy of Political and Social Science. 312: 116-26. Jl. '57. Diplomatic potential of NATO. C. K. Streit.

Christian Century. 74:1532. D. 25, '57. How NATO's role has changed.

Commentary. 28:207-13. S. '59. Tension in the Western alliance. Max Beloff.

Current History. 32:140+. Mr. '57. United States and a united West. Hans Kohn.

Current History. 39:129-68. S. '60. NATO and free world security [special issue].

Foreign Affairs. 36:278-92. Ja. '58. NATO: deterrent or shield? M. W. Hoag.

Foreign Affairs. 37:357-65. Ap. '59. New tests for NATO. P.-H. Spaak.

Foreign Affairs. 38:19-30. O. '59. France in the Atlantic community. René Pleven.

Foreign Policy Bulletin. 37:71-2. Ja. 15, '58. Changing NATO in a changing world. V. M. Dean.

Fortune. 57:98-103. F. '58. NATO alliance goes nuclear. C. J. V. Murphy.

*Harper's Magazine. 220.14+. Mr. '60. Editor's easy chair; the corpse on horseback. John Fischer.

*Listener. 61:620-1. Ap. 9, '59. NATO's tenth birthday. Sir Charles Webster.

*Listener. 62:1139-41. D. 31, '59. America and the defence of Europe. Michael Howard.

*NATO Letter. 7:1-7. D. '59. Political future of NATO. P.-H. Spaak.

Nation. 188:293-6. Ap. 4, '59. NATO: appraisal and forecast. Geoffrey Barraclough.

New York Times Magazine. p 19+. Mr. 8, '59. As urgent as the Moscow threat: strengthen the unity of NATO. H. A. Kissinger.

*New York Times Magazine. p 10+. D. 13, '59. If the U.S. does not lead. Drew Middleton.

*Réalités in America. 113:58-63. Ap. '60. What the West doesn't understand about de Gaulle. Maurice Schumann.

Reporter. 20:15-18. My. 14, '59. Backstage view of the alliance. Alastair Buchan.

*Reporter. 21:28-30. O. 15, '59. Wanted: a European deterrent. Alastair Buchan.

Reporter. 22:21-3. Ap. 14, '60. Should NATO become a nuclear power? Alastair Buchan.

Saturday Review. 43:10-12. Ap. 30, '60. How many worlds do we need? P.-H. Spaak.

U.S. News & World Report. 46:128. Je. 15, '59. Miracle of NATO. David Lawrence.

U.S. News & World Report. 47:57-60. N. 16, '59. NATO: shield or sieve? M. S. Johnson.

*United States Naval Institute Proceedings. 85:22-43. Ap. '59. NATO —keystone of defense. W. F. Boone.

Yale Review. 48:321-35. Mr. '59. NATO in the nuclear age. Lincoln Gordon.

IV. WORLD LAW AND WORLD GOVERNMENT

BOOKS AND PAMPHLETS

Bloomfield, L. P. Law, politics, and international disputes. (International Conciliation no 516) Carnegie Endowment for International Peace. New York. '58.

Brierly, J. L. Basis of obligation in international law, and other papers. Oxford University Press. New York. '58.

*Carnegie Endowment for International Peace. Perspectives on peace: 1910-1960. Praeger. New York. '60.
    Reprinted in this book: World commonwealth: a new look. Salvador de Madariaga.

Clark, Grenville and Sohn, L. B. World peace through world law. 2d ed. Harvard University Press. Cambridge, Mass. '60.

Corbett, P. E. Law in diplomacy. Princeton University Press. Princeton, N.J. '59.

Cousins, Norman. Who speaks for man? Macmillan. New York. '53. Chapter 27.

Jenks, C. W. Common law of mankind. Praeger. New York. '58.

Jessup, P. C. Transnational law. Yale University Press. New Haven, Conn. '56.

Jessup, P. C. Use of international law. University of Michigan Law School. Ann Arbor. '59.

Lauterpacht, Sir Hersch. Development of international law by the International Court. Praeger. New York. '58.

Lilienthal, A. M. Which way to world government? (Headline Series no 83) Foreign Policy Association-World Affairs Center. New York. '50.

Mangone, G. J. Idea and practice of world government. Columbia University Press. New York. '51.

Millard, E. L. Freedom in a federal world. Oceana. New York. '59.

Schwarzenberger, Georg. International law. Vol 1, 3d ed. International law as applied by international courts and tribunals. Stevens. London. '58.

Slick, T. B. Permanent peace; a check and balance plan. Prentice-Hall. New York. '58.

Thomas, Norman. Prerequisites for peace. Norton. New York. '59.

Visscher, Charles de. Theory and reality in public international law. Princeton University Press. Princeton, N.J. '57.

PERIODICALS

Bulletin of the Atomic Scientists. 14:259-61. S. '58. Only world government can prevent the war nobody can win. Bertrand Russell.

Current History. 39:65-113. Ag. '60. World federalism and free world security [special issue].

*Economist. 195:310-11. Ap. 23, '60. Up the world government path.

*Foreign Policy Bulletin. 38:135-6. My. 15, '59. Would world law avert war? V. M. Dean.

Life. 43:36. Ag. 12, '57. Liberty in law: how we got it and how we can extend it.

*Life. 48:35. Mr. 7, '60. Time to stand up for world law.

*Listener. 63:51-2. Ja. 14, '60. What is international law? R. Y. Jennings.

*National Review. 2:6-7. Ap. 25, '59. Mr. Nixon's nostrum.

New Yorker. 36:32-8. Je. 18, '60. Letter from the West. E. B. White.

Newsweek. 55:108. F. 22, '60. World peace by law. Raymond Moley.

Vital Speeches of the Day. 23:615-17. Ag. 1, '57. Freedom under law. H. L. H. de Kauffmann.

Vital Speeches of the Day. 24:295-8. Mr. 1, '58. World law or world holocaust. C. S. Rhyne.

*Vital Speeches of the Day. 25:421-4. My. 1, '59. Rule of law for nations; address delivered before the Academy of Political Science, New York City, April 13, 1959. R. M. Nixon.

V. CAN THE ARMS RACE BE CHECKED?

BOOKS AND PAMPHLETS

Aron, Raymond. On war. Doubleday. Garden City, N.Y. '59.

Baldwin, H. W. Great arms race. Praeger. New York. '58.

Halle, L. J. Choice for survival. Harper. New York. '58.

Kissinger, H. A. Nuclear weapons and foreign policy. Harper. New York. '57.

Melman, Seymour, ed. Inspection for disarmament. Columbia University Press. New York. '58.

Mezerik, A. G. ed. Disarmament: postwar through 1957. International Review Service. New York. '57.

Mezerik, A. G. ed. New proposals for disarmament. International review service. New York. '59.

Murray, T. E. Nuclear policy for war and peace. World. Cleveland. '60.

National Planning Association. 1970 without arms control. (Planning Pamphlet no 104) The Association. Washington, D.C. '58.

*National Planning Association. Nth country problem and arms control. (Planning Pamphlet no 108) The Association. Washington, D.C. '60.

Noel-Baker, P. J. Arms race. Oceana. New York. '58.

Nogee, Joseph. Diplomacy of disarmament. (International Conciliation no 526) Carnegie Endowment for International Peace. New York. '60.

Nutting, Anthony. Disarmament: an outline of the negotiations. Oxford University Press. New York. '59.

Rockefeller Brothers Fund. International security: the military aspect. (America at Mid-Century Series) Doubleday. Garden City, N.Y. '58.

Russell, Bertrand. Common sense and nuclear warfare. Simon and Schuster. New York. '59.

United States. Senate. Committee on Foreign Relations. Control and reduction of armaments; final report of the Subcommittee on Disarmament. (Senate Report no 2501) 85th Congress, 2d session. Supt. of Docs. Washington 25, D.C. '58.

United States. Senate. Committee on Foreign Relations. Controlling further development of nuclear weapons; collection of excerpts and a bibliography. 85th Congress, 2d session. Supt. of Docs. Washington 25, D.C. '58.

United States. Senate. Committee on Foreign Relations. Disarmament and foreign policy; hearings before a subcommittee, January 28-February 26, 1959, pursuant to Senate Resolution 31. Parts 1 and 2. 86th Congress, 1st session. Supt. of Docs. Washington 25, D.C. '59.

United States. Senate. Committee on Foreign Relations. United States foreign policy: Developments in military technology and their impact on United States strategy and foreign policy; a study prepared by the Washington Center of Foreign Policy Research, Johns Hopkins University. 86th Congress, 1st session. Supt. of Docs. Washington 25, D.C. '59.

Periodicals

Bulletin of the Atomic Scientists. 15:333-6. O. '59. Will a test ban treaty be signed? J. H. Spingarn.

*Bulletin of the Atomic Scientists. 15:361-5. N. '59. First things first. Eugene Rabinowitch.

Bulletin of the Atomic Scientists. 16:50-1. F. '60. Appraisal of the Geneva talks. Jay Orear.
    Reply. 16:186-7. My. '60. Scientist's non-scientific observations. John Lofton.

Bulletin of the Atomic Scientists. 16:85-8. Mr. '60. Nuclear test ban; symposium.

Bulletin of the Atomic Scientists. 16:181-4. My. '60. Nuclear tests and national security; condensation of report of Democratic Advisory Council's Committee on Science and Technology.

Business Week. p 126+. My. 14, '60. Why atom blast detection lags.

Current History. 33:193-246. O. '57. Disarmament and defense [special issue].

Foreign Affairs. 37:211-34. Ja. '59. Delicate balance of terror. Albert Wohlstetter.

Foreign Policy Bulletin. 39:103-4. Mr. 15, '60. Deadly nuclear game. V. M. Dean.

Foreign Policy Bulletin. 39:139. Je. 1, '60. Underground nuclear tests: pros and cons. Neal Stanford.

Fortune. 59:122-5+. Mr. '59. Nuclear inspection: a near miss. C. J. V. Murphy.

Harper's Magazine. 220:29-36. Je. '60. Politics for a new generation. P. F. Drucker.

New Leader. 42:6-7. My. 25, '59. Racing the bomb. Denis Healey.

New Leader. 42:11-12. Je. 8, '59. Danger of nuclear test bans. Reinhold Niebuhr.

*New York Times. p 3. Mr. 17, '60. 2 arms plans: how they differ.

*New York Times. p 20. Mr. 20, '60. Test ban parley a slow process.

*New York Times. p E 1. Jl. 3, '60. Arms impasse.

New York Times Magazine. p 11+. Ja. 5, '58. What hope for disarmament? H. H. Humphrey.

New York Times Magazine. p 9+. Ap. 19, '59. Why the Kremlin will not disarm. Chester Bowles.

New York Times Magazines. p 17+. O. 11, '59. Disarmament? The problem lies deeper. Salvador de Madariaga.

*New York Times Magazine. p 20+. N. 8, '59. Can we prosper without arms? S. E. Harris.

New York Times Magazine. p 7+. F. 14, '60. Russia and arms: a dark case history. H. W. Baldwin.

New Yorker. 36:32-8. Je. 18, '60. Letter from the West. E. B. White.

*Political Quarterly. 31:17-25. Ja. '60. Disarmament: dream or reality? Hugh Thomas.

Reader's Digest. 76:25-9. Ja. '60. What would total disarmament really mean? F. V. Drake.

Reporter. 22:20-3. Ap. 28, '60. Hopes and fears of an atomic test ban. C. M. Roberts.

Science. 131:1298-9. Ap. 29, '60. Enforcing an atom test ban: scientists testify before Joint Atomic Energy Committee.

*Time. 75:26-7. Ap. 11, '60. Test-ban primer.

U.S. News & World Report. 48:116. Mr. 28, '60. Disarmament blackmail: Soviet plan. David Lawrence.

Vital Speeches of the Day. 26:205-8. Ja. 15, '60. Dismantling of the era of terror. T. E. Murray.

VI. UNDERDEVELOPED NATIONS: THE NORTH-SOUTH PROBLEM

BOOKS AND PAMPHLETS

Berliner, J. S. Soviet economic aid: the new aid and trade policy in underdeveloped countries. Praeger. New York. '58.

Buchanan, N. S. and Ellis, H. S. Approaches to economic development. Twentieth Century Fund. New York. '55.

*Hoffman, P. G. Interdependence—fact and opportunity; address to the Chicago Rotary Club, December 15, 1959. The author. United Nations Special Fund. New York. '59.

Hoffman, P. G. One hundred countries, one and one quarter billion people: how to speed their economic growth—and ours—in the 1960's. Albert D. and Mary Lasker Foundation. Washington, D.C. '60.

Kenen, P. B. Giant among nations; problems in United States foreign economic policy. Harcourt. New York. '60.

Myrdal, Gunnar. Rich lands and poor; the road to world prosperity. Harper. New York. '57.

Organization for European Economic Cooperation. Remodeled economic organization; report by the group of four. The Organization. Paris. '60.

Rostow, W. W. Stages of economic growth. Cambridge University Press. New York. '60.

Sapir, Michael. New role of the Soviets in the world economy. Committee for Economic Development. 711 Fifth Ave. New York 22. '58.

Staley, Eugene. Future of underdeveloped countries; political implications of economic development. Harper. New York. '54.

Stanford Research Institute. Significant issues in economic aid to newly developing countries. The Institute. Menlo Park, Calif. '60.

*United States. Senate. Committee on Foreign Relations. United States foreign policy: U.S.S.R. and Eastern Europe; a study prepared by a Columbia-Harvard Research Group. 86th Congress, 2d session. Supt. of Docs. Washington 25, D.C. '60.

PERIODICALS

Current History. 37:233-8. O. '59. Economic competition in the underdeveloped areas. A. Z. Rubinstein.

Foreign Affairs. 38:31-45. O. '59. Operation Breakthrough. P. G. Hoffman.

Fortune. 59:104-7+. Ap. '59. Good uses for $750 billion. G. H. Burck and Todd May.

Fortune. 60:135-8+. D. '59. Stages of growth as a key to policy. W. W. Rostow; with reply by D. M. Wright.

*New York Times. p 36. Ap. 13, '60. Russia's cold war battle plan. C. L. Sulzberger.

New York Times Magazine. p 23+. My. 22, '60. Cold war that is only beginning. E. L. Dale, Jr.

Saturday Evening Post. 232:42-3+. My. 14, '60. Economic revolution. Barbara Ward.

*Saturday Review. 43:20-5. Ja. 16, '60. New international balance: challenge to the Western world. Sir Oliver Franks.

United States. Department of State Bulletin. 40:750-8. My. 25, '59. United States and the challenge of the underdeveloped areas of the world. F. O. Wilcox.